49-Year-Old

Virgin

Delayed, NOT Denied

Dr. Paula C. Perez

DrP & Me, LLC

Scripture quotations marked (KJV) are taken from the KING JAMES VERSION, public domain.

Scripture quotations marked (NIV) are taken from the Holy Bible, New International Version®, NIV®. Copyright © 1973, 1978, 1984, 2011 by Biblica, Inc.™ Used by permission of Zondervan. All rights reserved worldwide. www.zondervan.com The "NIV" and "New International Version" are trademarks registered in the United States Patent and Trademark Office by Biblica, Inc.™

Scripture quotations marked (AMP) are taken from the Amplified Bible, Copyright © 1954, 1958, 1962, 1964, 1965, 1987 by The Lockman Foundation. Used by permission.

Library of Congress Control Number: 2022918538
ISBN: 979-8-9870016-0-8 (paperback)
ISBN: 979-8-9870016-1-5 (audiobook)
ISBN: 979-8-9870016-2-2 (e-Book)
ISBN: 979-8-9870016-3-9 (pdf)
ISBN: 979-8-9870016-4-6
(workbook *Delayed, Not Denied: A Christian Relationship Guide*)

Praise for 49-Year-Old Virgin

[Perez] broaches a topic that is often considered taboo for discussion in the church world. Dr. Perez talks about celibacy, which is an ideology, for some in the secular world, that is often thought to be old-fashioned and irrelevant. However, she describes her journey with such humanity and warmth, until I found myself wrapped in a blanket thoroughly drawn into her story. I was able to envision the places [the author] visited as she writes as though she is living in the very moment and provides every detail. Her accounts of encounters with people who helped or hurt her left me feeling as though I either loved them or felt disdain for them. For me this book is about family, faith, and freedom. Paula says out loud what she believes, and her family supports her faith. Dr. Perez believes what she has spoken into the universe will come to pass, and it does. The *49-Year-Old Virgin* will free women and men of all ages from the notion, "You've got to try it, before you buy it."

~ Evangelist Sharon Henderson,
Elect Lady Powerhouse St. Luke COGIC,
Morris Park, New York

This new book was such an inspiration to read. I felt like I was a part of her family and ready to cheer her on. This book also made me reflect on certain aspects of my own life, family dynamics, and choices I made. It made me remember how faithful God is in our walk with him. I hope this book will be an inspiration to others who read it as much as it was to me.

~ Pat Weatherspoon, Houston, Texas

"[A] must read … It touches on many of the day to day temptations that we all deal with. Many of us are not fortunate enough to have held on to or kept our virginity until marriage. The author expresses how so many times she could have lost hers, but the power of prayer and a good village and standing strong on God's words is what helped her. I really recommend this book, especially for teenagers and women who are still fighting to remain a virgin.

~ Adrienne Jenkins, Poughkeepsie, New York

… An inspiring, encouraging, and uplifting book that gives an account of what God can do in your life in spite of any and everything you have gone through. It inspires you to live and keep living a life that pleases God. It encourages you to pick yourself up and dust yourself off after being disappointed. It uplifts you to know that God knows what your heart's desire is and what you dream of. Also, it lets you know that God's plan and his desire for you is greater than anything you could ever design for yourself and he has the power to make it come to pass. This book is an informative guideline and resource on how to navigate life in order to get to a happily-ever-after ending. This is a must read.

~ Lisa Silver, Ossining, New York

To anyone wanting to
save themselves for marriage
or wishing they had waited,
you too can
change your sexual legacy

Contents

Foreword

Whr I met Dr. Paula Perez about a year ago and heard a little of her story, I was amazed and knew there was something special about her. Weekly in my relationship sessions on "celibacy," she would come and share just a bit of the story. Each time, she would share a little more detail. It became evident that she was a woman of conviction and strength. She was very transparent and touched my heart and hearts of the other women. A 49-year-old virgin? How honorable! Her commitment to God, respect for family, and tenacity to push through temptations and challenges encouraged us that we, too, could succeed on our celibacy journeys. When she shared that she was writing a book, I knew I wanted to be one of the first readers to experience the fullness of this incredible story.

After reading this heart wrenching memoir in which Dr. Perez recounts her life of sexual purity and self-discovery, all I could say was, "Wow, what a journey!" I have often made a statement about the biblical story of Job, that his story was not about him but more about God. His story started with God choosing him and ended with God blessing and restoring him . . . but oh, the journey! The journey was unbelievably and painfully rough. When I read this memoir, I found myself with the same sentiments, although I dare not and do not compare the two stories. However, Dr. Perez's journey is her story, but her story is about God! God had a plan for her life, and God's plan prevailed ... but oh, the journey! The journey was a long and rough delay. But as you will read, it was not a denial. It was worth the wait!

I love that this memoir is carefully written and not only highlights Dr. Perez's joy and pain but also showcases the love of her parents and family. They faithfully supported her along the way. On the celibacy journey or any major endeavor, you cannot make it alone. You need a strong support system to listen, correct, encourage, and hug you when the heartache seems unbearable. Dr. Perez had times of heartache but had many people to lean on. They assured her of God's loving plan and to hang in there!

Have you vowed to abstinence or celibacy until God sends your mate? Do you want to be celibate but not sure you will endure? Have you tried and failed and given up? Maybe it's not a mate. What are you waiting on from God? Whatever it is, Dr. Perez's story of love, family, faith, courage, heartbreak, tears, resilience, and joy will inspire you to be patient with God. Wait on God! He has a wonderful plan for your life and will not disappoint you. Just as this 49-year-old virgin did, commit your ways to God and trust Him on the journey. Do not allow what seems like a delay or denial to get you off the path. There is a reward and joy waiting for you, and it will be worth the wait!

~ Janice J. Burton, The Marriage Planning Mogul
Author, Speaker, Relationship Coach
www.doithebook.com

Part 1

Prelude to the Journey

S tanding there staring at my petite, five foot one chestnut-brown frame in the mirror, I thought, *Not bad for a forty-nine-year-old virgin.* It was hard to believe that it had been thirty-three years since that fateful day when I committed to saving myself for marriage. The journey wasn't always easy, but I was committed to my choice of remaining a virgin until I married. I just never thought I would still be waiting!

People today can't imagine the concept of saving oneself for marriage. We are bombarded by sexual images and the expectation that everyone is doing "it." The prevalent view of sex is that it's part of adulting. The statistics are abysmal in this area, even among people who say they are Christ followers.

Sadly, as an educator, an administrator, and a preacher's kid, I have witnessed the devastation and fallout of peoples' decisions to have sex outside of marriage. Their actions have resulted in broken hearts, dashed dreams, and unfulfilled potential.

Unexpected pregnancies have fostered guilt and added to the statistics of children in single-parent homes being shuffled between households. "Daddy issues" surface because of the absence of the father. But it does not have to be this way.

I'm living proof that everyone is *not* doing it. I believe there are others like me, who want this different experience. Even though we are living in a hypersexualized time, it is possible to remain celibate until marriage.

However, I have to admit, I thought I would marry within four or five years of getting out of high school, like my parents. After all, I loved Jesus, faithfully served in church, obeyed my parents, and was a "good" person. Of course, I thought I would go to college, earn a degree, and leave with my MRS title too.

Boy, was I wrong.

I will share my experience through the pages of this memoir. As you read, reflect on your own life. Then jot down your own feelings and connections to my story, in the *49-Year-Old Virgin: Delayed Not Denied Notebook.* Create a free account; then download the notebook for free from my website: https:drpaulacperez.com/resources-for-you or by scanning the QR code.

Chapter 1

THE DECISION

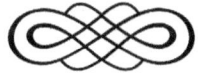

My unexpectedly long journey began during the summer of 1976, at a seminar that I had no idea would so fundamentally alter the course of my life. That June, several families from our church headed to the Jersey Shore. The weeklong Institute in Basic Youth Conflicts (IBYC) seminar was being held again in Ocean Grove, New Jersey. My family and I had attended the year before and had thought it was great. So, we encouraged the parishioners to come with us this year.

At the seminar, I had learned that most adult issues stem from unresolved childhood conflicts. I had also realized that God is more concerned about developing my character than my temporary happiness. I looked forward to learning even more while I was at the conference this year. But first, we had to check into the bed-and-breakfast. When we passed the Pink Flamingo Hotel, we knew we were close.

***

The air in the auditorium, built before air conditioners were common, was stifling. Our church group found chairs near the windows. Although the air was hot, we could feel the occasional breeze. I wished I had brought my pillow, but once the speaker started, my attention moved from the pain in my butt to the presenter.

The auditorium, filled with people of every hue, was packed. It was wonderful to see all the mothers and fathers as they settled into their seats with their families.

Only one person spoke the entire conference. The speaker knew how to tell a story. He looked small on the stage, but they projected his image onto two theater-sized screens that made it easier to see. He always wore the same type of clothes: a black or navy blue suit with a handkerchief, white shirt, tie, and patent leather shoes. He was clean-shaven with a short haircut fit for a salesman or politician. He was small in stature, but his voice filled the room.

Sitting with my red notebook and pen in hand, I followed along as he gave us the words to complete the fill-in-the blank worksheets. He taught on everything from the necessity of forgiveness to the importance of choosing the right friends. Tonight's topic was relationships.

The speaker wanted us to realize all relationships start with us and the way we view ourselves. We must recognize who we are and who we belong to. I am a Master's original, a King's kid.

He emphasized the importance of choosing qualified life partners and the role of fathers and father figures in this process:

"I'm asking every father in this auditorium to please stand. Fathers, you have a responsibility to your children," he said. "You are to protect them until they enter into a covenant of marriage with their life partner. Tonight, fathers, daughters, and sons, I challenge you to enter into a covenant with each other and God. Make the decision to wait for God's choice for your life. If you are willing, turn to the back of the book and complete the agreement."

I turned to the back of the book and saw "A covenant between a father and daughter as witnessed by the Lord Jesus Christ. We agree together to seek God's best concerning a future life partner."

The man up front continued speaking. "Fathers, do you commit to protect your daughter from unqualified men and to teach her God's principles of life? Will you pray for her and for God's choice of her life partner? If you do, please sign on the line. You may be seated.

"Sons and daughters, do you promise to keep yourself pure for your mate? Do you vow to obtain your father's blessing on your courtship? Will you wait for your full release before entering into marriage? If you do, please sign your name on the page."

That day, my father and I both signed the covenant. All of my life, my parents taught me about how special sex was and what a gift it was to maintain my virginity until marriage. Over the past five years, since I gave my heart to Jesus, I had grown in my faith. Through a series of events, the Lord proved to me that he was real. My desire was to please him. When the presenter challenged us to make the commitment to remain virgins until marriage, my heart was open to receive the message. I wanted to please my heavenly Father. I wanted to please my parents. I wanted to please my future husband. Thus began my commitment to remain a virgin until marriage. It was a commitment that would last far longer than I expected.

Chapter 2

THE SETUP

Thirty-two years later, I found myself still single and living in the basement of my parents' home. However, I loved my life. My family and I were close. I had two completely different careers, one in corporate America, and the other in education. Over the years, I had visited thirty of the contiguous states and Hawaii. I also traveled to Canada, Mexico, England, and New Zealand.

I was still active in our church. Every Sunday you would find me teaching Sunday school, conducting kids' church, and singing on the praise team, and choir. I was also very committed to working with the women.

In the fall of 2009, I hosted an intimate women's retreat for thirty women at a hotel fifteen minutes outside of Albany, New

York. The hotel, approximately fifty minutes from where I was born and still lived, was in the Catskill Mountains.

Although it was a week before Thanksgiving, the hotel was already decked out for Christmas. The building was covered in lights. As we walked into the lobby, the smell of burning wood and the warmth of a real fireplace greeted us. Two cozy chairs and a couch were perched in front of the fireplace. The scene was inviting. In the middle of the room stood a spiral staircase with a wrought iron banister. The hotel boasted several Christmas trees spread throughout the facility. To the left of the entrance door and directly across from the fireplace stood the check-in counter. As we entered, the clerk welcomed each of us to the hotel.

I had worked on this retreat for months. As my guests began to arrive, I felt an air of anticipation. Perhaps it was because of the various messages I heard at church, but my faith was strong. I believed something special was going to happen that weekend. I had no idea that the excitement would result from words that I would put into the atmosphere. Nor could I grasp that the words I spoke would change the trajectory of my life, but they did. At this small, cozy affair, I declared, "I'm going to get married within the year."

Wait, did those words actually leave my mouth? Did my internal dialogue become my spoken words? Yes, I said the thing out loud.

"What did you say?" Alaina asked.

That was my good friend, Alaina, one of my trusted confidants. We met when she moved to the area ten years earlier with her son to become an assistant principal at a middle school in a neighboring district. Alaina was a slightly lighter version of

Academy Award-winning actress Octavia Spencer, with the same style and grace. We became friends right away. She joined our church shortly after we met, mostly for her son's sake. We had a lot of boys his age, and Alaina felt our church was an environment where he could learn the same biblical tenets she did as a child. Eventually, she became a part of our church and the small group I hosted for single women. We often traveled to concerts and went to plays together.

For a period of time, Alaina and I both worked as administrators at the local school district's central office. The shared experiences dealing with our colleagues definitely brought us closer together. We spent hours in each other's offices, laughing, crying, and praying together.

"Did you say you're getting married? To whom?"

Well, that was the thing; I didn't have a boyfriend. I wasn't even seeing anyone. No viable candidates were on my radar, and she knew it. However, I held on to the prophetic words spoken to my dad by a visiting minister two months earlier. It happened at my dad's church one Sunday morning.

On that Sunday, my sister, parents, and I were in our spots on the stage, as usual. My sister and I were in the choir, which was always situated center stage behind the speaker's podium. My parents and other special guests sat in their chairs on the platform, stage right. Their section faced the side of the podium.

"Is there a street named Magic here? Who lives on Magic?" Prophet Weaver asked.

My sister, parents, and I looked at each other, then walked toward the speaker near the front of the stage. He turned and looked at us as we approached. I gestured to the speaker that it was our family that lived on the street. My niece, who was out in the audience, joined us on the stage.

"You're getting ready to receive a son-in-law. He's a man who's holy."

As he said that, the crowd erupted with clapping and cheering, thanking the Lord. Although neither my sister nor I were married, I claimed the prophecy for myself. I did a happy dance right there.

Then turning and speaking directly to my father, the prophet said, "The spirit of success is on his life." He continued. "God is preparing him now; but his greatest success is being yoked to your daughter. He will only receive the favor that he needs by being around the overflow of favor in your daughter's life. 'He that findeth a wife findeth a good thing and obtaineth the favor of God.' I see right now, this man has been in the presence of God, and God is working on him. He's preparing him, and you ain't gonna have to worry about nothing. When she's out of your house, she's gonna stay out, in the name of Jesus!"

His words took root in me, began to sprout, and then blossomed, causing me to move into action.

During that year, I took a sabbatical and left my administrative position in the school district to open and operate my own private preschool, King's Kids Early Child Development Center, an extension of my after school King's Kids community program. I became a morning person, rising before dawn to head to the gym to get my body in shape. As a result, I started getting up at 5:30 a.m. to get to the gym before I reported to work at 7:30. I went to Planet Fitness and worked out for an hour before

I went to the church to open up the preschool. I wanted to be ready for my photos at my impending nuptials so I sought out an orthodontist to fix the gap that had formed between my teeth because I stopped wearing my retainer shortly after getting my braces off in high school.

The sabbatical I took from the school district also allowed me the time I needed to work on myself from the inside out. I needed to remember my "why." The time off allowed me to delve into books. I read my Bible, *Start with Why* by Simon Sinek, *Showing Mary* by Renita J. Weems, Rick Warren's *The Purpose Driven Life*, and *The Shack* by William P. Young. Each of the books spoke to me and helped to strengthen my faith and inner self.

During that time, I worked on strengthening my relationship with the Lord. It was nice working out of the church because after the kids left, I could pray and seek God alone in the sanctuary. I lived on a steady diet of Joyce Meyers and T. D. Jakes, along with my own church services. Yes, I prepared my mind, soul, and my body. After all, I had to be camera ready for my upcoming wedding. And now, all the women knew that I was expecting this miracle too.

Chapter 3

DIVINE APPOINTMENT

S/even months had gone by since I made my pronouncement. Now it was the last day of the school year. Teachers were finishing up their reports, clearing out their personal items, and submitting their final requisitions to me. I could finally take some time to relax and do what I wanted to do. Once the last teacher left the building, I headed home too.

Hmm, maybe I'll go to the Fourth Saturday Conference. It was held each month in Harlem. This event brought together church members from across our jurisdiction for the purpose of training and equipping us to do ministry. Because of my hectic school schedule as a principal, I wasn't able to go for several months. But now that school was over, I felt a need to start going again.

"Hey Dad, can I get a ride with you guys tomorrow?" Dad was sitting in his usual spot in the sunroom—right beside Mom in their matching brown reclining chairs. The two of them were seldom apart. Theirs was a love affair that started while they were still in their teens, but now his beard was gray with decades of experience.

Dad was fine with it with one caveat: I had to be ready and in the car when he pulled out. He was the conference president, and arriving late was *not* an option. I assured him that I would be ready. The last thing I wanted to do was drive to New York City by myself.

***

"No, no, no, no . . ." As I reached for my glasses, the position of the hands came into focus. "That clock can't be right. How did I oversleep!" *Bang!* The front door slammed. "Oh man, they left me. They really left without me! Why didn't they wake me up? They knew I wanted to go."

I had such a sinking feeling. But in that next second, I realized I did not have to accept defeat. I could do something about it. I immediately thought about my Uncle Ramon. *Maybe he is still home*, I thought. He had been married to my dad's sister Laila. Even though she died decades earlier and he had since remarried, he was still family to me.

"Are you going to the conference today? If so, can I get a ride with you?" I anxiously awaited the answer from the other side of the phone. My desire to get to the conference was undeniable. I waited. The answer was yes. My uncle told me he would be at the house in thirty minutes.

Uncle Ramon's house was downtown. It would only take him about fifteen minutes to drive to our house in Cherry Hill. I knew

I had to hurry. *Hmm, now, what to wear? Thank God, I picked up my dry cleaning.*

I pulled out the freshly cleaned and pressed black dress with white polka dots, jumped in the shower, then quickly got dressed. "*Whew*. Just in time." I could hear the car pulling into the driveway.

Looking out the window, I could see the sun as it beat down on his balding head. He was cloaked with his clergy garb. The black shirt with the white clergy collar around his neck reminded me of a choker necklace.

By the time we arrived at the venue in Harlem, the parking lot was full. So, he dropped me off in front of the door. It was a gorgeous summer day, Saturday, June 26. As I opened the door, the sunlight poured in from behind, enveloping me in the frame of the door.

The smell of bacon, eggs, and grits met me like the embrace of an old friend. The cafeteria was packed. I surveyed the dining area and finally spotted my parents. They were finishing up their breakfast. As I approached the table, their faces showed it all. They were shocked to see me.

"Did you drive down by yourself?" Dad knew I hated driving in the city, especially by myself.

"No, Uncle Ramon drove me down. He's parking the car."

"Grab a chair and pull it up to the table," Mom said.

I pushed a chair next to my mother's and then stood behind the last person in line so I could grab some breakfast. As soon as I got in line, I saw Elder Perez. I knew the Ridges would not be too far away. As I peered over his five foot eleven inch frame, I saw them. Elder Ridge was Elder Perez's pastor and spiritual father. Elder Perez served as his armor bearer.

I admired how he looked out for them. He usually chauffeured them wherever they needed to go. He tended to their needs so all they had to do was concentrate on their assignment. Little did I know, I would benefit from this character trait in the future. I quickly grabbed my food and rejoined my parents at their table.

I was so thankful that we arrived in time for breakfast. With the morning rush, I did not have a chance to eat. As I looked at the clock, I realized the conference was getting ready to start. It was almost 10 a.m. When I think back on that day, I can't help but wonder, "What if . . .?"

Part 2

Links Between the Ages

We inherit from our ancestors gifts so often taken for granted—
our names, the color of our eyes and the texture of our hair, the
unfolding of varied abilities and interests in different subjects . . .
Each of us contains within our fragile vessels of skin and bones
and cells this inheritance of soul. We are links between the ages,
containing past and present expectations, sacred memories, and
future promise. Only when we recognize that we are heirs can we
truly be pioneers.

—Edward Sellner

Before I dig deeper into my story, it is important for you to know a bit about my extended family. I have a rich family history. Like every family, some of the history is good and some is not. Despite how the past is classified, my great-grandparents, grandparents, and parents forged a path for me to live out my single years empowered by the lessons learned from their experiences.

Chapter 4

CASEY, NELLIE, AND MOMMA TOO

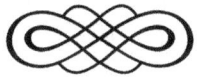

It was 1936. At sixteen, my grandfather Casey was already living a very different life than the one I chose to live at that age. He was already a father. You have to realize that in 1938, Judeo-Christian principles were still the norm. People were looked down upon when they had a child out of wedlock. Now it was time for Casey to have a reckoning with his mom.

"Don't tell me that girl's pregnant again. I've had it. Boy, what's wrong with you? You're seventeen, and you already have three kids, with three different women, and another on the way! You better marry this one," Pert said as she peered over her wireframe glasses. She was only five foot two inches and 120 pounds. Next to Casey's lumbering frame, she seemed even smaller, but he still had a healthy fear of her.

"But, Ma, you know I want to play baseball in the Negro league. I won't be able to do that if I'm strapped down." His large, brown eyes longed for her to understand his point of view.

"Well, you should've thought about that before you put your penis in her again. That is not the way your father and I raised you. You have to make this right. You hear me, Junior? You better get a job and start supporting your kids! Marry her before that baby is born!"

Sure, he liked Thelma. She was beautiful, outgoing, and always wore stunning clothes, no doubt the benefit of having a mother who was a seamstress. Even after having their first baby, she maintained her hourglass figure. Although he slept with and impregnated two other women, Casey knew Thelma still loved him.

Casey wasn't sure what to do or say, but his mother, Pert, put her foot down. She was a strong, God-fearing woman from the south. Pert was one of the best cooks in the region. She knew how to read and write too, which was not the norm at the time. As the eldest in her family, she was used to raising kids because she helped raise several of her siblings. Pert glared at Casey until he complied with her wishes. He knew she was not putting up with any more of his nonsense.

Thelma was the mother of his first child, Glenda. "OK, I'll marry her," he said, obediently fulfilling his mother's desires.

About a month later, and before Thelma's second pregnancy was noticeable, Casey married her. He got a job with the state, building roads. Thelma and Casey welcomed Elizabeth, their second child together (and his fourth in total) into their tiny apartment just a few months later.

In 1939, less than a year after Elizabeth was born, they realized they were pregnant again. Thelma already had two girls. She desperately wanted to give birth to a son. Thelma was well aware that Casey had two sons by two other women, but she wanted a son to call her own. She would name him Jesse.

Throughout the pregnancy, Thelma prayed that it would be a boy. Finally, the day arrived.

"Aww. My water broke!"

"Thelma, come lay down here," Pert said as she carefully warmed water over the flame. She already had some rags that were ready. Pert, Casey's mom, had insisted on coming to the house as the due date drew near. Thank God she did. She would have missed the birth, and Casey and Thelma would have had to fend for themselves.

"*Shh*, it's okay," Casey said, pacing back and forth holding Elizabeth, their second daughter. Thelma's screams had startled her.

"God, it hurts," Thelma said.

"It will be over soon. Just breathe and push!" her mother-in-law, Pert, said.

With one last push the baby popped out on Sunday, April 28, 1940. Thelma and Casey welcomed their third child together.

"What is it?"

"A healthy girl!" Pert said.

Thelma sighed. Hmm, we'll have to come up with a girl's name. After a day or so they settled on: Darcy Jesse Clara Jean Daw. That daughter, Darcy, grew up to become my mother.

The Glasco apartment was too small for Thelma and Casey's growing family. About a year after Darcy's birth, Casey and Thelma moved into his parents' house at 30 Tompkins Street in Kingston, New York.

The house was a mansion in comparison. A large living room was downstairs and at the rear of the house, a big kitchen. You accessed the backyard through the back kitchen door. Unlike the other place they lived, the bathroom was inside. Three bedrooms were on the second floor. In 1941, with Casey off to war, it was a great comfort and help for Thelma to have her in-laws in the house. By this time, Casey and Thelma had three children under five years old with a fourth child on the way.

Thelma and Casey established a pattern. Almost like clockwork, every two years from 1936 to 1948, they had a child. They had six girls in twelve years: Glenda, Elizabeth, Darcy, Evelyn, Rene, and Shelby.

Chapter 5

GIRL TALK

D ar, my mother, told me that a byproduct of growing up in a house full of girls was that sex was often a topic of discussion. She said they discussed everything openly and honestly. They talked about the need for boundaries in the area of sex. When reminiscing about her past, Mom talked about my maternal grandmother, Thelma, having a green book. It was their go-to resource on human anatomy. I found it really interesting that in the 1950s, my grandmother was so open about sexuality. You would think in this decade that would have been a taboo topic. However, according to my mom, they could ask her anything. I guess that experience helped to shape my mother, because my mother developed the same type of open communication with my siblings and me.

Mom explained that her parents set boundaries. My mother and her sisters had a 9 p.m. curfew. However, her parents exhibited a great deal of trust in them. This allowed my mom to make decisions for herself. She went to the neighborhood parties at the chippy joint. It was a safe environment for the young people to hang out. Alcohol was not allowed, but Mom had no plans to drink, smoke, or have sex anyway.

I wonder if her decision was influenced by her parents' lives, like my relationship decisions are tied back to my parents' influence on my life.

Yes, my maternal grandfather and grandmother had children before they married. My mom saw how their choices limited their opportunities. My grandfather's dream of playing in the Negro baseball league went unfulfilled. Darcy also observed the influence of alcohol and smoking on her family's life.

My grandfather was usually a quiet and reserved man. However, when he was intoxicated, he transformed from mild mannered to the incredible hulk. My mom recalled that his entire gait changed when he was under the influence. When he was under the spell of the spirits, he was a different person.

My mom, Darcy, still has a scar from stepping in between her father and mother when Casey went after Thelma with a knife. She protected her mom, but her payment for her heroism was a trip to the hospital to get stitches.

I'm sure all of this played into my mom's determination to stay away from alcohol, sex, and cigarettes. In her mind they went together. She had no desire to continue the pattern of substance abuse and kids out of wedlock. Mom envisioned a different path. The idea of losing control was repellent to her.

Mom disciplined herself to study and work hard. Throughout her schooling, she excelled. As young as elementary school, she held offices in clubs.

In elementary school, she received the award for having the highest grades in the school. In middle school, she went to the city and played her violin at a music festival. By her senior year, she was first chair and played with her orchestra at the famed Carnegie Hall in New York City.

No one in her family ever went to college. Mom decided she would be the first. She joined the Future Nurses of America Club in high school. As long as she could remember, she always wanted to be a nurse. With her gift of helping others, nursing was a perfect fit.

My mother definitely passed her passion for education on to me. She would tell me, like her mom said to her, "If other kids could do it, you can too." Years later, I would climb to the highest heights in education and earn my doctorate degree.

Chapter 6

SHH . . . DON'T TELL ANYONE

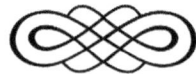

Across town, the woman who would become my paternal grandmother and her parents had to deal with a different type of drama. Let's pick up her story in 1937, shortly after she turned sixteen.

The city where my great-grandparents lived still had its share of segregation in 1937. Yes, it was the North, but the Southern ways were there too, like cockroaches under the floorboards. So when migrant workers came from the South to find work, they took refuge in the homes of other Negroes, including my great-grandparents' place. It was much cheaper and safer for the laborers to stay with their own kind.

I don't know if my great-grandparents ever thought about these strangers and their possible impact on their family. Perhaps it was a simple economic decision for them. The "rent" money the tenants paid—a quarter here, a dime there—came in handy and helped put food on the family's plates. However, it cost Nellie, my grandmother, so much more.

***

"Momma, can I go down to the beach?" Nellie asked. The proximity to the river was the benefit of living on River Road South.

"Yes, but make sure you're back in time to help with dinner. The workers will be hungry, and I want to make sure we have plenty of time to prepare everything so it's ready when they return."

My great-grandma, Pam Palmer, was a thin, medium-build woman in her late thirties. She was known as Momma. The wire frames of her glasses sat on the bridge of her nose, just enough so she could glance over them. Momma's most unique feature was her crippled left hand. It was bent inwards with her fingers almost touching her wrist.

"Leave your sister Lillie here. I need her to help me with something," she answered. The house was crawling with boarders. They came from the South in search of jobs. The brickyard, which was near the public beach in Ponchonkie, provided the hope of an honest living. Each summer a different crop of men came by car, bus, train, and foot to find work. That's why my great-grandfather, Billie Palmer; his wife, Pam; and the kids initially moved from South Boston, Virginia to the area. They all came with the dream of making a lot of money.

As my father, Jay, began to tell me the story surrounding his birth, my mind tried to fill in the missing pieces of what might have happened to my grandmother Nellie.

I imagined that Nellie was glad she could go down to the river and even happier she didn't have to bring her little sister Lillie. All Nellie could think about was cooling down her body. The sun beat down on her head like a hot, dull hammer. She had a headache from all the pressure. The air in the house was even hotter than the summer sun. It was stifling, and the natural remedy was a dip in the cool river.

Nellie ran toward the crashing waves. As she stepped into the cold water, her pace decelerated. Like weights clasping on to her ankles, the water slowed her stride. Her eyes focused on the concentric circles in the water. Perhaps that's why she didn't notice him at first. Caught up in the blissful peace of the moment, she waded out and submerged her body.

I bet Nellie relished the opportunity to have some space to herself. If their house was anything like it is now, it was always crowded with neighbors and friends; but with the summer tenants, peace and quiet was nearly impossible to find.

Suddenly Nellie felt a touch on one of her arms, startling her and disrupting her serene space. Nellie quickly stood in the water. She recognized him. He smiled at her. Nellie smiled back.

As she turned her back to move away, he grabbed her from behind. In one motion, he put her in a hold, wrapping his arm around her from behind and covering her mouth.

She struggled to get free, but her sixteen-year-old body was outmatched by his 200-pound frame. He dragged her out of the water and threw her on the sand. Her wet body hit the ground with such force, the pain shot through her head. She thought she saw stars. He yanked on her bathing suit. It was a one piece, so it was harder to take off than he anticipated.

Once again, she attempted to escape, but he forced her back down in the sand. As she continued to try to fight him off, he pulled down her bathing suit. Suddenly, she felt a pain like she had never experienced down there. She felt something running down her leg. It might be the water, but she wasn't sure. He kept thrusting himself into her body. When he finally rolled off her, she just lay there with a mixture of tears, mucus, and sand running down her face.

"*Not a word to anyone*," he said. Then he vanished almost as quickly and quietly as he came.

After lying on the ground for a moment, Nellie slowly got up and looked around to see if anyone was there. Then Nellie walked the lonely path home.

"I was a product of rape," my dad said. "It was one of the tenants, but they never told me his name. My mom was sixteen when I was born."

As my father, Jay, recounted his birth story to me, I wiped away the tear that rolled down my cheek. I was twenty-nine, and it was the first time I heard the story. But Dad had just recently heard the story himself. One of his sisters pried it out of my grandmother Nellie. That was not a topic that Great-Grandmother Pam nor Grandmother Nellie ever discussed.

It was hard to wrap my head around it. I can't imagine the weight of the trauma my grandmother experienced. I wanted to ask more about the rapist, but instead I asked about something I came across in the 1940 census. "Why did they list you as Great-Grandma Pam's son instead of Grandma Nellie's?"

On the 1940 census paperwork I discovered, the census taker wrote down that the head of the household, Billie Palmer, was born in South Boston, Virginia. He had a third-grade education. At the time of the census, he was forty years old.

They wrote that Pam Palmer, his wife, and his daughters were also born in Virginia. Great-Grandma Pam had a fourth-grade education. She was thirty-eight years old. They had two daughters Nellie (eighteen years old) and Lillie (twelve years old); a son, Jay, who would grow up to be my father (two years old); and a grandson, Jeremy, one month old.

"Well, I was a very sickly child. My mother was only sixteen when she had me. She didn't know what to do with me, so Grandma Pam stepped in and assumed the role of mother. I don't know, maybe the census taker just assumed I was her son instead of her grandson. Regardless of the reason, I grew up calling my grandmother Momma and my mother, simply Nellie."

Dad went on to explain that his mother, Nellie, got pregnant with Jeremy while she was engaged to marry Bernard, Jeremy's father. However, a few days before the wedding, he enlisted in the army and was shipped out to war. My grandmother, Nellie, was devastated that she was violated again. The emotional scar of being stood up was difficult for her. She was eighteen and longed to be loved.

It seemed like the men she entered into relationships with all preyed on her vulnerability. Fitz was the next man to come into her life. He told her how beautiful she was and made her feel special. His charm worked on her. She allowed Fitz to get her into bed too. She hoped things would be different with him, but they were not. At nineteen, Nellie was pregnant again, this time with Fitz's baby. He vowed he would marry her, but once again, Nellie was denied. For the second time, she was left at the altar. Incredibly, Fitz also joined the army and left Nellie holding a baby and her broken heart.

From her sexual encounter with Fitz, she had a daughter, Laila. Nellie, now with three kids, felt she needed to change her life. She turned to a relationship with Jesus Christ for healing. She vowed she would not allow another man to touch her until he said *I do* at the altar. She remained celibate for three years. That's when she met, fell in love with, and married Chip. Nellie was twenty-three.

When Grandma Nellie got married to Chip, the only child that she moved in with was her daughter Laila. Laila was three at the time. My grandmother Nellie left her two older kids, my father Jay (seven) and my uncle Jeremy (five) with their grandmother Pam.

Many years after I learned more about my grandmother's story, my father also shared that the scar of this abandonment was difficult for him. My grandmother had five more children after she got married. All of his siblings knew their fathers and had a relationship with them, but my dad never did. Then his own mother left him behind with his grandmother. Momma, as Jay called his grandmother Pam, was indeed his mother.

Despite the rejection my father, Jay, faced, he was still surrounded by a village, a neighborhood that loved and supported him. They looked at his report cards and praised him

31

for his accomplishments. Likewise, if he got in trouble, the neighbors were there to chastise him.

"We had a group of friends that hung out. You know, like the little rascals," my father said. "If you saw a picture of us from back then, that is exactly what we looked like. We were mischievous. I believe the Lord saved me when I was eighteen to keep me from wrecking my life! If I continued with my stealing and lies, there's no doubt I would have ended up in jail. Thank God for redemption!"

By sixteen, my father had been the "man of the house" for three years. My dad explained that his grandfather Billie was a kind man with a quiet spirit. With barely a third-grade education, Granddaddy Billie was illiterate and did not know how to count money. Daddy explained how he came to assume that role.

"When I was about twelve, I overheard a bill collector on the phone yelling at my grandmother, Pam. I took the receiver from her and told that man, 'I'm the head of this house. Don't you ever call up here yelling at my grandmother like that again. You speak to me!' From that moment, I assumed the role of bill payer for our household. I found jobs shining shoes or helping at the neighborhood store to assist my family.

"By the time I was eighteen, I knew I wanted to have a family. I knew what type of father I wanted to become too. I would be involved in my children's lives. They would know I would be there for them. My eighteenth year was a pivotal one for me. First, IBM came to the high school to recruit students to work at the newly built plant. I was one of the fortunate students that were hired. Secondly, I started dating your mother, and then Jesus transformed my life. I asked Jesus into my heart and that changed the direction of my life!"

Chapter 7

LET'S ELOPE

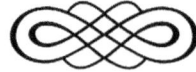

When my mom was sixteen, she was also committed to remaining a virgin; however, she had already met the love of her life.

My parents—Jay and Darcy—started dating after her sixteenth birthday. My dad was eighteen. As with many first loves, their emotions were intense. By the time Darcy was ready to graduate from high school, they had been together, on and off, for two years. They committed their undying love to one another.

"Let's get married after you graduate."

"I don't know what my parents will say."

"Well, let's talk to them anyway."

My father, Jay, had a great relationship with Darcy's parents. They liked him a lot. Jay even taught Casey, my mom Dar's father, how to drive. He was always at their house.

My grandfather Casey liked to joke with Jay. Thelma and Casey had put their girls on a strict curfew, so Jay knew he would see one of her parents when it was close to the time for him to leave. Casey would often come downstairs to get a drink of water out of the kitchen. He would point to his watch as he looked at Jay. Then he would ask something like "So, what was the hymn from Sunday?" or "What scriptures are you going to read at service?"

My grandfather knew Jay, my dad, was a minister. But that did not stop Granddaddy Casey from trying to get a little help with his illicit gambling from God. I think Granddad thought if he played numbers tied to a Bible verse or a hymn number, that he would gain favor from the Lord. Clearly, Grandad Casey's intentions were not spiritual. My dad knew this was one of Grandad's tactics for selecting which numbers to play, but Dad went along with the game anyway.

But on this evening, before Casey could ask, Jay spoke first. "Darcy and I want to ask you and your wife something. Would you please ask Mrs. Daw to come down."

"Thelma!"

"What?"

"Come down here!"

A few minutes later, Thelma came down the steps to the kitchen.

"Mr. and Mrs. Daw, you know how much I love your daughter. May we have your permission to get married after she graduates this year? I have money saved from my IBM job. I plan to get another part-time job.

"Negro, you're just in heat. Get over it. You're not getting married until she finishes college."

"Darcy, you have been talking about going to college to become a nurse since you were a child. We want you to accomplish your dream first. Besides, you know they don't allow married women at Albany Medical Center," Thelma said.

As quickly as Jay asked, my mom Darcy's parents dashed their dream of marriage. It was 1958. People expected married women to stay home and take care of their husbands and children. Darcy's parents wanted more for her. They wanted her to achieve her dream first. Although this delayed their nuptials, they were not denied.

After graduating from high school, Darcy went to Albany Medical Center to get her nursing degree while Jay enlisted in the reserves to fulfill his military duties.

While Jay was stationed in San Antonio, Texas, they wrote every week, keeping the flames of their love alive. Once finished with basic training, Jay returned home.

By the beginning of 1961, Darcy was almost finished with school. Graduation was just five months away. They could finally get married. They were so excited!

***

However, they didn't want to wait for a formal wedding. They just wanted to get the ceremony over. Besides, with the money they would save doing it this way, it would help them to rent an apartment and begin their life together. So, they made plans to elope.

"Sally, may I borrow your dress; you know, the green one?" Darcy asked.

"Sure. When do you need it?"

"Friday morning. I'll give it back to you on Monday."

"Oh. I thought you wanted it next week. I need it Friday, I'm going out."

"No problem."

"What did you need it for?"

"That's okay, I'll find something else." With that, the phone rang. "Hello"

"Hey Babe. Are you all set for Friday evening?" Jay asked.

"Yes. I can't wait!" The phone was in the hallway of her dorm room, so she dared not mention their plans out loud.

"Dar, I have the license. Great news, my sister Laila and her boyfriend said they would stand up with us."

"That's great. Babe. I have to go. Someone is waiting to use the phone. I'll see you Friday." With that she hung up the phone with a big sigh, trying not to show her disappointment. Now what am I going to wear, she thought. The only clothes she had that looked dressy was her black dress. Well, that will have to do.

Their marriage was almost five years in the making. Jay picked her up and drove to the church in Albany. The two married, Friday February 10, 1961. Dad's sister Laila and her boyfriend were their witnesses. Mom graduated a few months later in May. Fortunately, by graduation, Darcy still was not showing signs that she was pregnant with me. She didn't have to explain to the school, or her parents, that she was married and then got pregnant before graduation. I was born later that year in October.

Part 3

Train Her Up

I grew up in the 1960s and 1970s. I was blessed to be surrounded with a large extended family. All my grandparents, with the exception of Great-Grandma Pam and her husband, Great-Granddad Billie Palmer, lived within blocks of one another in Ponchonkie.

The Palmers lived in a senior citizen apartment complex on the other side of town.

It was always so funny to me to watch the expression on the clerks' faces when we went into the store and asked them for five Mother's Day cards—one for each of our grandmothers and a sixth for my mom. I did not know anyone else that grew up with five grandmothers who were still alive in their lifetime. We knew we were blessed.

However, the men in our family did not fare as well. I knew my paternal great-grandfather, Billie, and my paternal step-grandfather, Chip. I also knew Granddad Casey, my mom's father. However, the rest of my grandfathers died much younger. This influenced my decision about the age of the guys I eventually dated. All of them, with the exception of one, were younger (more about that later).

For a period of time, my great-grandmother Pam actually moved in with us at my parents' home. She lived with us after Granddaddy Billie went into a nursing home. By this time, I was in high school. Thankfully, I did not experience the death of any of my grandmothers until I was twenty-nine. All five of them died in their nineties!

Although my family provided stability in my life, I grew up in America in a time of great civil unrest. The country was in an unpopular war in Vietnam. Black women were finally given the right to vote. I recall the feeling when I went to the polls with my mom for the first time. It was exciting. I also remember marching uptown with my parents and others in protests over civil rights in our city. Even though we were in the North, they did not serve Negroes at the lunch counter at our Woolworth's store either.

My earliest memory was of the day when John F. Kennedy was shot. We were having my sister's first birthday party. I do not remember what was said, but I do remember the television and the feeling that something was wrong. Sadly, this was the first of many assassinations in the 1960s. Other political and civil rights leaders who also met untimely deaths at the hands of someone else: Medgar Evers, Malcolm X, Martin Luther King Jr., and Robert Kennedy, to name just a few.

During this same time frame, the first man landed on the moon. I ran home from a piano lesson to watch the event on our black-and-white television in our living room. So much was going on in the world!

Woodstock, the famed outdoor concert that lasted several days, took place about twenty minutes from our house. With the technological advances in birth control, women were liberated. It was a sexual revolution, a time of bra burning and open sexual activity. Sex outside of marriage was no longer taboo and instead was encouraged by pop culture. This was the backdrop of my life during my formative years.

As a result, my parents were very deliberate in how they brought my siblings, Ann and Brian, and me up. There is no doubt in my mind that my parents' experience with their families also shaped the type of parents they desired to be. Our family unit has always been a top priority in their lives.

My mother earned her nursing degree and became a registered nurse. My dad worked at IBM and decided to go back to college when I was just starting kindergarten. They both worked second shift when we were little, so our dinner times were sacred. It was the time that my parents used to pour biblical principles into us. As the eldest child, they practiced on me.

My parents were determined to teach us about Christ so that when we were old enough, we could decide for ourselves to follow Jesus. As the eldest child in my family, naturally I was the first to experience their teaching tactics. However, more of my lessons were gleaned from observing them than by listening to what they said.

The five of us sat around the table. Dad sat in his chair at the head and Mom in her seat at the opposite end. We usually ate dinner around 3:30 p.m. because both my parents worked the second shift. Dad was still at IBM, and Mom worked at Benedictine Hospital.

We had a ritual of practicing Bible verses at the dinner table. The card holder, colored in shades of tan, looked like a loaf of bread with the middle cut out. Instead of doughy bread, there were a hundred different colored rectangular cardboard cards, with Bible verses written on them. I took a card but couldn't read all the words. Mom took it and read it first. I repeated what she said.

"'Remember your Creator in the days of your youth, before the days of trouble come and the years approach when you will say, "I find no pleasure in them."' Ecclesiastes 12:1. Now you say it." Mom then excused herself from the table to change into her nursing outfit.

I repeated the words until I could quote them from memory.

Then Dad asked me to recite John 3:16. If I got it correct, he gave me the card. If I got it wrong, he kept it. I loved this game.

"'For God so loved the world, that he gave his only begotten Son, that whosoever believeth in him should not perish, but have everlasting life,'" I said, "Yes," pumping my fist, "I won again!"

Just as I finished reciting the verses, Mom reemerged, ready for work. Right on cue, the doorbell rang. It was our babysitter. The amazing thing is, I still remember the verses I learned as a child.

Chapter 8

NOW, LET'S TALK ABOUT SEX

I first learned about sex when I was eleven. I'll never forget the experience. We lived in our old house on Hasbrouck Place.

My mother, Darcy, brought me into the dining room and talked with me as we sat on the radiator. I don't think I was ready for the conversation, but obviously she did. I think it was due to her upbringing with a family of girls. She was also pregnant with my youngest sibling. Her body became an object lesson and visual aid as my brother grew and expanded inside her. She came equipped with the technical jargon and diagrams too. This was the benefit of being a nurse. She had access to a lot of free materials.

She explained that every living thing has a reproductive system. Mom asked me if I knew the purpose of the reproductive system. I did because I had learned about it in science class.

"To have babies."

She then explained that when a man and a woman come together and connect, it is called sex. My mother told me it was important that I remember that God invented sex. Just like everything God made, it was good.

I knew she was telling the truth. Those words were in the Bible. I also saw a book on the shelf in their bedroom with the red and white title on the cover. It was titled *God Invented Sex*. I learned when I was older that it was written by Charles E. Wittschiebe.

"Remember, everything that God created was good, including sex," she continued. "When God made man and woman, he said it was 'very good.' As your body grows and develops, certain things will start to happen. You will get taller, your hips will get wider, hair will start growing in different places on your body, and you will get your period." She then explained the menstruation cycle. This was strange to me and a little scary too. I wondered if it was a lot of blood. I just hoped my cycle wouldn't start too soon.

Mom explained that the penis goes into the vagina. *How the heck does that happen?* I thought. I could not figure it out, and Mom did not make that part clear.

Pointing to our good dishes in the china cabinet in the dining room, Mom continued by saying, "Just like we do not use these dishes every day, just on special holidays, that is what God wants us to do with sex. God invented sex as a special activity reserved for married people. Just like we save these dishes for special occasions like Thanksgiving and Christmas, that is what God wants us to do with sex—wait until you are married.

"Yes, sex is fun. It feels great. When you have it, you will want to have it all the time. God designed it this way on purpose. It is one way to help husbands and wives create a strong bond that would make them want to stay together. It is a demonstrative way for married couples to show their love for one another. That is why they call it 'making love.' When you and your future husband connect in this way, it will make you even closer," Mom said.

I did not ask her any questions. I could not imagine a boy being that close to me. A few weeks earlier, a boy tried to kiss me on the way home from school. I slapped him. I certainly was not letting any boys get close enough to me to do that!

I learned a lot that day, but I came away with more questions than when we started.

Chapter 9

MAKE A CHOICE

*All your righteousness would have no influence to uphold you
or keep you out of hell any more than a spider web can
stop a falling rock.*

—Jonathan Edwards

s I grew up, my parents continued to teach us Scripture, pray with us, and take us to church. In 1969, my dad became our pastor, but also maintained his job at IBM. By this time, my mother was working the first shift. Although I knew a lot about Jesus, I still had not decided to follow him. I think my parents assumed that I had already made the decision to follow Christ.

One day after school in 1972, I had to walk home by myself. My siblings, Ann and Brian, got picked up early because they had an appointment. When I got to the house, I called out to Mom. I ran up the porch steps and through the front door, past the living room, and straight back to the kitchen. I saw on the stove that dinner was already in progress. Steam poured out of the cast iron pots. I called out for her again. "Mom!"

Maybe she was upstairs. Before leaving the kitchen, I turned to my right and peeked into the dining room. Nothing. I turned around and ran back the same path I just traversed, looking quickly to my left to see if she was in the living room—still no sign. *Where is everyone? Brian? Ann?* I turned to my right and darted up the two flights of stairs to the second floor. I looked down the hallway. *"Mom!"* Still no sound. I turned to my left and looked in the bathroom. The bathroom was empty.

My heart raced. It was now beating so loudly that I could hear it through my chest cavity. *This is just like the movie,* I thought. The images from *The Thief in the Night,* a Christian movie that my dad showed us at church, were still vivid on the screen of my mind. This Technicolor film, set in the early 1970s, opened with the ticking hands of a yellow old-fashioned alarm clock. On the screen appeared the warning: "'Keep a sharp look out for you do not know when I will come, at evening, at midnight, early dawn, or late daybreak. Don't let me find you sleeping.' Signed, Jesus Christ."

Although I was the "good," compliant first-born, I also knew none of these things would get me into heaven if I had never asked Jesus into my heart.

Did this game of playing church get me played? Did Jesus come and go without me? Was I left behind? A million questions flew through my mind in just a few seconds, as did the memory of the theme song from *The Thief in the Night* movie. The theme song haunted me. I'll never forget the melody.

At that moment, my mother appeared. I have no idea where she was, but the relief was palpable. "Mom!" I ran and hugged her. *Thank God, it was not the rapture.*

I never shared my secret thoughts with my parents. They had no idea that I thought the rapture had happened and I was left behind because I never asked Jesus to forgive my sins. As a PK, I knew they assumed I was already a born-again Christian, which would save me from the penalty of hell. I didn't want them to know I was not saved. I planned to make the decision when I was older. Even though I knew I could be left behind, it wasn't enough to move my eleven-year-old body forward to actually make the decision to follow Christ. This required a near death experience and a vivid description of hell.

Chapter 10

UNCOVERED

I was good at playing church, but up to this point, I still had not "become the church." However, that would soon change. I was twelve years old, in the sixth grade, and about to be revealed.

We were in Sunday school, and my mother was our teacher. To this day, I cannot remember exactly what I said, but I remember my mother's words.

"I thought you loved Jesus?"

That silenced me. It felt like Mom could see inside my heart. She exposed my secret, revealing that I was not a Christian. I never admitted that I was a sinner. I never asked Jesus to forgive me for my sins. Nor had I accepted Jesus's generous gift of salvation. Jesus voluntarily died on the cross for me to save me from eternity in hell. Not once had I confessed that Jesus was

Lord of my life and that I would live my life according to his principles. So, I spent the rest of the class only answering questions when she called on me.

After Sunday school was over, we went upstairs for the church service. Elder Sutherland preached the sermon. I remember his ebony skin. He wore a black suit with a white shirt and a skinny black tie. He seemed much older than my parents, but he was probably only five to seven years older.

He titled his sermon "Receive the Gift."

"God loved you so much, he sent his son Jesus to die in your place. Every one of us was born in sin, and our penalty for that is death. If you die without Christ, you'll be doomed to hell," he said.

After the service, Dad stayed with Elder Sutherland at the church while Ann, Brian, and I went with Mom to drop off a visitor from Teen Challenge, a Christian-based addiction rehabilitation program in Red Hook. It was still snowing when we left. Mom drove up the street, took a left, and then after passing three streets, she took the next right up First Avenue. As we started to turn left toward Dinkies Pond, a car came from around the curb and careened into our path. It was headed right toward us!

"Jesus!" was all Mom could yell. There was no time for a lengthy formal prayer, but this short one sufficed. Miraculously, the car slid past ours without incident.

I cannot die—I do not want to go to hell! That's all I could think as we drove the rest of the trip. Between my mom realizing that I never asked Jesus into my heart, Elder Sutherland's sermon, and almost getting killed in a head-on collision, the Lord had my attention.

After dinner, we went back to the church for part two of the revival service with Evangelist Sutherland. He was even more passionate at the evening session.

"I'm telling you the truth. If you walk out of here without Jesus in your heart, you may not make it back. If you die, from hell you will lift up your eyes.

"A few years back," he said, "I was in Rochester, and I gave the invitation to Christ. I saw the spirit of death on a young man sitting in the back pew of the church. 'Young man. Yes, you in the back. God is telling you your time is running out. I beg you to give your life to Christ right now. If you walk out these doors without asking Jesus into your heart, you will not make it back in.'"

The evangelist continued. "It grieves my heart to report that the young man ignored my pleas. He left the service early. As I prepared to give the benediction, someone ran into the church to tell us that the young man was dead. As he got out of his car to go to a party, he was struck by a car. It killed him instantly. Don't let that be your fate. The devil wants you in hell with him. Receive Christ before it is too late!"

With tears in my eyes, I walked to the altar and stood in front of the preacher. Others came too, but I focused on myself. I did not want to go to hell. I did not want to be left behind. Instead, I made a choice. I chose to serve Jesus.

Chapter 11

A MATTER OF FAITH

After I decided to follow Jesus, I began to grow in my understanding of God's Word. When I first accepted Christ, it seemed like the Lord answered all of my prayers. I viewed God as a loving father. This was easy for me because of the relationship I had with my own father. Because of my own dad's love, I could envision God in the same way. I'm sure he granted my request as a means to increase my faith. However, nothing solidified my faith like my father's death experience in September 1977. Yes, my father dropped dead. It was shortly after he and my mother returned from a business trip to Europe.

Dad sat in the pulpit area with the guest speakers. Aunt Laila, on her post at the piano, had a clear view of them from the piano.

After my father introduced the guests, he went back to his seat.

Suddenly, Aunt Laila frantically waved to get Mom's attention. We had no idea what she was doing. She was always calm, never animated. Once she got my mother's attention, she motioned to where my dad was sitting. Because we were listening to the speaker, we hadn't noticed that Dad had slumped down into his chair.

It took a moment for my brain to register what was happening. It was not until Mom jumped out of her seat, grabbed Dad, slammed him to the floor, and started chest compressions that I realized the severity of the situation. Dad was not breathing. I started crying.

Fortunately, my brother Brian immediately ran downstairs to call for an ambulance. This was before the advent of cell phones and the 911 system. He had to locate the phone number, then physically dial the number using a rotary phone. Once he reached someone on the phone, they made him get an adult to confirm that it was truly an emergency. All of that took time.

Suddenly, out of the chaos, we heard the voice of the evangelist. "Saints, why are you crying as if there is no hope? I told you earlier this week that God was going to do a miracle. This is why we fasted and prayed. Call on God. Stop crying and pray," said the evangelist.

Everyone started shouting to the Lord. There was no formality, just intense prayers to give our pastor, leader, father, and husband back to us.

My grandmother and aunts ran up the street when they got the news. They could not handle another death in the family. Earlier that day we buried Grandma Nellie's sister-in-law.

It took approximately twelve minutes for the ambulance to arrive. One of the paramedics had gone to school with Dad and knew him. They relieved Mom and started doing CPR. While all of this was going on, the people in the church continued to pray. "Lord, heal our pastor. God raise him up! Bring him back to life, Lord!"

The paramedics continued working on him. Although there was no sign of life, I think they knew if they didn't do something, they would have to contend with an emotional crowd.

They removed him from the pulpit area and placed him on the stretcher. They began to roll his lifeless body out of the sanctuary. At that moment, my life without my father flashed before my eyes. *No. God, this can't be happening.*

As the paramedics neared the door, my father slightly moved, then his eyes opened. There was a pulse. It was weak, but he now had a pulse. They stopped rolling the stretcher and put an oxygen mask on his face before placing him in the ambulance. My mother followed behind and went with them in the ambulance to the hospital.

The people in the church began praising God for the miracle we just witnessed. They were joyful, but I was scared. I was not sure he would make it through the night. My siblings and I went to Aunt Laila and Uncle Ramon's house to await word from Mom. None of us slept.

After several hours, the phone rang. Aunt Laila answered the phone. It was my mother.

"Laila," Mom said. "It looks like he's going to make it, but they want to keep him and run some more tests. They're not sure what happened."

The next day, Dad's manager from IBM visited him in the hospital. After they exchanged greetings, Dad told him he was through with the job. Time was too short, and he needed to work full time for the Lord. He was going into full-time ministry.

Al, his boss, tried to talk him out of his decision. He encouraged my father to take some time off and not to make any rash decisions. He reminded my father that I would be starting college in two years. Then behind me, I had three other siblings that would need to go to school.

My father thanked him, but told him he felt the Lord wanted his full attention. He was giving up the job and focusing his energy on the ministry.

His boss would not accept his resignation. Instead, he put him on paid leave for the year. He said they would revisit the conversation in a year.

A year later, my father officially retired. The Lord proved that he was a provider. Because my father put God first, the Lord took care of all of our needs. In the words of Matthew, "But seek ye first the kingdom of God, and his righteousness; and all these things shall be added unto you" (Matthew 6:33 KJV).

***

I turned sixteen a couple weeks after my father's "death" experience in the service. That experience increased my faith in the power of prayer. But I have to admit, those first few weeks after Dad came home from the hospital, it was as if I was holding my breath. I was waiting for confirmation that he was really out of danger. By week three, I realized I had finally relaxed the muscles in my body. I no longer felt the need to stay on high alert. Dad was okay.

Thankfully, things were back to normal. Good thing too—I was celebrating my sixteenth birthday in a few days. I was finally old enough to get a real job.

The day after my birthday, Mom agreed to pick me up from the YMCA. That's where we went to get our working papers. I couldn't wait to get them. Not that I had much choice. My mom would have signed me up when I was six if she could! That was about the age I started doing chores. But I had to admit, I liked the idea of working a real job.

The next stop was to fill out an application at Waldbaum's Grocery. I applied for a cashier position. When I submitted the form, the lady at the counter said the manager was not available, but she would give him my application.

The first week went by, and then a second. I wondered why I had not heard from them yet. As I thought about it, I had a strong feeling that I should call them and ask about the position.

"Hello. May I speak to the manager?" I asked.

"How can I help you?"

"I called to find out if I'm on the schedule for this weekend."

"Hold one second." After about five minutes, the manager returned and said, "I don't see you on the schedule, but why don't you come in on Saturday. We'll get you started."

It worked, it worked! Oh, my goodness, I didn't even have an interview. I could not believe I was hired without even meeting the manager in person. I laughed as I relayed the story to my parents.

In that season, I felt like a baby taking my first faith steps. Sometimes I faltered, but encouraged by those around me, I picked myself up and started again. With each victorious outcome, my faith increased. I was learning to trust God. It was a good thing, because I would need to rely on this faith to navigate future relationships.

Chapter 12

THE AWKWARD STAGE

B y the time I was sixteen, in 1977, I was in tenth grade, my first year at the high school. It was a real struggle. Most people don't realize it, but I am an introvert. I have to force myself to engage with new crowds. Over the years, because of the countless recitations, speeches, songs, and plays, I had gotten used to being in public. However, in new environments, my insecurities are more prone to appear.

My first year of high school was very challenging. I was placed in the college prep courses. I was often the only Black student in my classes. If there was another Black student, it was one of my cousins. Tracking practices were prevalent in our school. Most of the other Black students were placed in "school level" classes, which were the lowest track.

I was five foot one inch, extremely skinny, with glasses and buck teeth. I laugh now, because when my parents said I needed braces, I did not want them. Thank God they were in charge! The hardest part of the day was walking to the cafeteria. I hated the daily barrage of catcalls from the guys that lined the hallway. Instead, I spent my lunch period in the library or at Aunt Laila and Uncle Ramon's house. That was a much safer choice for me as I hated how the guys rated the girls' bodies as we walked pass them. My body was finally going through the changes Mom talked about when I was eleven, but I was still pretty flat-chested. Later that year, my period finally started.

I epitomized a late bloomer. Despite my prayers, my boobs just did not pop out, I'm sure, in part, because of all my physical activity. We were always playing softball, kickball, and touch football. It was not uncommon for us to ride our bikes around town too.

Chapter 13

PUPPY LOVE

He was the star athlete of the basketball team, the team's point guard, tall, fast, and precise. He spun around his opponents on the court like it was nothing, putting up shot after shot. I thought he was the most handsome guy around. Just the way he smiled and looked out of the corner of his eye made the butterflies in my stomach rise to the top of my rib cage.

It's crazy how we got together. I knew Lamont all my life. So throughout childhood, we just hung out. We loved to play kickball, touch football, and baseball. I was one of the guys.

The year I became a junior, our feelings changed from friendship to really liking one another. I cannot say a specific time when he asked me to be his girlfriend. We just grew into it. I loved him as much as a teen could.

Because of our new relationship, I looked forward to going to lunch at school now. I no longer wanted to hide out in the library or at Aunt Laila's house.

Lamont and I always had lunch during the same period. We sat at the same table with our friends and played games with each other. As Lamont put his head down on the table, I leaned over his back and wrote "You're my man" or "I love you" with my finger. With each letter, Lamont gave me a sign that he knew what I was writing. Then we would switch places.

Lamont taught me how to French-kiss in the basement of our old house while the adults were upstairs having Bible study. I loved when he kissed me. We had to sneak to do this. No public displays of affection were allowed in school or at home. So, to get away from peering eyes, we often left school and made out in the cemetery. Sometimes we did some "grinding," but always fully clothed. We never talked about actually having sex. I had recently made my decision, in front of my parents and the rest of the crowd in Ocean Grove, New Jersey, that I would remain a virgin until I got married. I guess I assumed that Lamont felt the same way.

Our church always had a lot of excursions. One of our favorite trips was to Storytown, an amusement park in Lake George. The bus left early in the morning and usually returned close to midnight. Lamont and I always sat toward the back so it was easier to steal a quick kiss. My heart rate quickened with just the thought of his soft lips kissing mine. We snuggled in the back of the bus under a blanket. Once the lights were off, and we heard the rhythmic snoring of the older folks, we knew it was safe.

The drill was the same when we went to youth crusades or other church events. However, when Uncle Ramon drove the van, it was harder. It's a wonder he stayed on the road. Much of the time his eyes were in the rearview mirror looking back at us. When it was dark outside, we never knew when he might turn the lights on in the van. But we took the risk anyway.

That summer, I couldn't believe Mom and Dad let me go with Lamont and the crew to the United National Auxiliaries Conference. There were seven of us in total: three girls, two guys, and two dads that served as our chaperones. UNAC was held in New Orleans at the Superdome. We had a great time.

Lamont and I held hands as we walked side by side. His afro was always perfectly trimmed with every hair in place. He usually placed his pick in the center of his afro. I loved his fishnet shirts. They allowed me a peek at his muscular brown body.

I know this sounds crazy, but at the time, I never thought about having sex with him. Even though I enjoyed the kissing sessions, my mind never entertained the thought. In addition to the vow I had made to remain a virgin, my mother provided my other reason. Since my mother got pregnant with me right away, I was always fearful that the first time I had sex I would get pregnant. The fear factor was one thing that kept me on the straight and narrow.

Lamont and I never talked about marriage. However, he was the male lead in all my dreams. Of course, I was going to marry Lamont, my first love. But that all changed when I heard about the pregnancy.

He had gotten another girl pregnant. Did he get her pregnant on purpose? I don't think so, but it felt like he was looking for an excuse to break things off with me. I guess he wanted to explore his options. Maybe it was because I was getting ready to go away to college. Well, having a baby with someone else was a sure way to bring a relationship to its end.

***

"After the Love Is Gone," the Earth, Wind, and Fire song, blared on the radio. My whole body ached as I cried myself to sleep that night. I hated him for leading me on. Now I understood what people meant when they said there is a thin line between love and hate. *Didn't Lamont know how much I loved him?* We never discussed it, but I assumed Lamont felt the same way I did about sex. I thought he also believed that sex should remain in the boundaries of marriage. *Why couldn't he wait till we got married?*

"Lord, he has to know I'm the one for him."

After that, the Midnight Storm on the radio became the soundtrack of my life. Every break-up and make-up love song they played resonated with me. The tears flowed. When Peaches and Herb's song, "Reunited," came on the radio, I cried even harder.

"With one perfect fit, baby this one is it." Why couldn't Lamont see that we were a perfect fit? God, please fix this!

I have always been a romantic. As a teen. I loved watching TV shows like *Gidget, The Sound of Music,* and *Cinderella.* Perhaps it was my flair for the dramatic, but I tended to overreact. As the distance provided by time grew, I realized my reaction with Lamont was over the top. I would survive. Life would go on.

Part 4

My Path

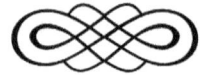

"The Lord protects the simple . . ." (Psalm 116:6 AMP). I believe the Lord looked at my heart and saw my intentions. He knew I desired to please him. When my flesh was weak or just too naive to understand the situation, he stepped in and protected me. He provided a way for me to escape.

Chapter 14

So Naïve

L amont and I were not meant to be. Now it was time for me to consider my college plans. I was not sure what I wanted to do with my life. When the chance came to attend a special program geared to getting women and minorities into the engineering field, I took advantage of the opportunity.

So, the summer before my high school senior year, I spent three weeks at Rensselaer Polytechnic Institute. During that summer program, I decided I would study engineering in college. That July, I applied for early acceptance into RPI, and I got in. As a result, before my high school senior year started, I knew I was going to RPI. Now the moment was here.

As a senior in high school, I won over ten scholarships. Since my parents wouldn't have to pay as much for college, I expected to find a car in the garage after my high school graduation, but that did not happen. Consequently, it was my parents' car, not my own, that rolled up to Davidson Hall, filled with my luggage, dorm room accessories, and my family. All five of them drove me up to say goodbye as I started my college career.

This dorm space was a major step up from the quad where I stayed the previous summer. Instead of one big room with bunk beds and four people, this dorm space had a common area with double rooms off it. What I loved about it was the partial wall that separated the double room into two spaces. You could actually have some privacy in the space. We also had a private bathroom in our room, similar to a motel bathroom, instead of the common bathroom shared by everyone on the floor like we did in the quad.

My roommate wasn't there when we arrived, but it was evident that she was already settled in. Her space was the first one we saw when we opened the door. My area was to the right of the partial wall.

I assured my parents I would be fine. "You guys can go; I know you have church tonight."

"Slow down. I know you're ready to get rid of us, but before we go, let's have a word of prayer," Mom said.

My father began to pray and ended it with "Lord, help her to be a missionary rather than a mission field. In Jesus's name, amen."

This was something my parents often said to the young people at our church. Their years of experience let them realize that the decision to follow Christ is made up of daily decisions. If we do not actively live our lives in this way, we may open ourselves to attacks from the enemy's camp, Satan. In a weakened state, we are more prone to accept things that are contrary to the Word of God, such as sex before marriage.

After hugging my parents and each of my siblings, we said our final goodbyes. As soon as they left, I put up my clothes, then left in search of my friends. I quickly connected with upper classmates that I had met the previous summer: Tony, Peter, Elaine, Melody, and Shay.

Less than 1% of the student body was Black, so we clung to one another for support. Instead of the school's student union, we hung out at the radio station and our unofficial "Black Student Union." This was a house off campus. It was our space, a place where we did not have to perform. We could let our guard down and be our authentic selves. In this judgment-free zone, we could take off our masks and get off the stage. It was safe.

My first five months on campus, I didn't attend church. I think I was trying to exert myself as an adult. Like a lot of young people who grew up in our church circles, church attendance was one of the first things we rebelled against. Prior to going to college, I went to church five to seven days per week. So, my first act of freedom was to stop going. When asked, I said I attended Pillow Pentecostal, a cute way of admitting I didn't attend anywhere. It was a stark contrast to my life before college. The first couple of times, I really felt guilty. However, I soon pushed the feelings aside.

When my mom wrote and informed me that the church was coming up for a fellowship service at St. John's, Elder Jack's church, I decided I better make an appearance. So, about a month before my dad's church was due to come to Albany, I started showing up at St. John's. I wanted to make sure if asked, Elder Jack and others could confirm that they saw me in services. I just hoped they wouldn't ask how many services.

***

I was excited when Shay invited me over to his apartment. He was one of the guys I met when I was on campus the previous summer. The night started with a few of us playing games and watching TV. Soon the others left, leaving me alone in the apartment with Shay.

Shay motioned for me to sit next to him on the couch. As we watched the movie, I laid my head on his shoulder. Shay put his arm around me and started kissing my earlobe. Then he moved to my neck. We soon went from watching TV to kissing on his couch. All of the sudden, he jumped up.

"You got to go! You got to go!"

"What?"

"Go-home-Paula!"

I gathered my things and left. At the time, I had no idea what was going on. Now I know he sent me home to protect me. I think the Lord made him stop. Thank God he watches over widows and fools, for clearly, I was in the latter category.

The next evening, student affairs showed a movie on campus. A bunch of my friends decided to go.

"Why don't you come with us, Paula?"

"Where?"

"To see Richard Pryor's *Live in Concert* film."

My eyes must have revealed my ignorance. I had no idea who Richard Pryor was, but before I could ask, one of my friends continued.

"He's a comedian."

It sounded harmless enough. I rationalized that since they were showing it on campus, it wasn't like I was really "going to the movies." Growing up, going to the movies was off-limits. I think it was the organization's way of keeping us from becoming polluted with the ways of the world. The only movies I watched were shown in church or on TV. You have to remember that when I was growing up, TV was not like it is now. There was no such thing as streaming services. We only had three basic channels—ABC, NBC, CBS—and WPIX, the local channel. *The Honeymooners* aired on this station.

So, I joined my friends. Let's just say, my virgin ears were not ready for the dose of comedy he doled out. Don't get me wrong; I laughed so hard, tears rolled down my face, but I also had moments when I felt very uncomfortable. I had no idea the movie was rated R. *Note to self: you cannot handle R-rated movies.*

This experience made me recall a time when I was flipping through the television at night and came across a couple on a rooftop. The man hoisted the girl up on the wall and began thrusting himself into her. I couldn't turn the TV fast enough. Those five seconds are forever embedded in my brain. I believe that's when I realized I just couldn't watch those types of movies. Believe me, a lot of prayer and fasting was required too.

After the movie, we headed to one of the dorms, where they were having a party. As I started to pick up a glass of punch, Shay said, "Girl, don't drink that!" With that, he took the glass out of my hand.

"Why?"

"It's spiked. It has alcohol."

I was grateful how, throughout my freshman year, God surrounded me with friends who looked out for me. Once again, Shay played the role of protector.

Prior to this, I never even had a sip of alcohol. Even for communion, our church organization used grape juice rather than wine. I had no desire to drink. It was not appealing to me. I had no desire to light up a cigarette either. I guess the idea of putting something in my body that made me lose control or made me sick made no sense. I'm sure the fact that I never saw my parents with alcohol or cigarettes also played a role in my decision. They did not allow it in our house. By this time, my maternal grandfather, Casey, did not drink any more either. He gave it up when he committed his life to Christ. The Lord completely transformed his life. He no longer desired to drink or smoke.

***

The course load was heavy. My freshman year I took physics, Calculus I and II, chemistry, computer programming (Cobol, Fortran), and sociology. My sociology teacher was an atheist. Throughout the semester, he challenged the existence of God. Even though I knew I wasn't doing all that I should, my belief in God was unwavering. I witnessed his influence in my life and in the life of my family too many times to doubt him. My sister, Ann, was healed. My father came back to life and years later, was healed from prostate cancer too. No, I couldn't see God, but I saw evidence of his impact everywhere. I could feel his presence in my life.

By spring semester, I realized a few things. I wanted to be saved, not just because that is what my parents expected of me, but it was what I wanted for myself. I decided to live my life according to God's plan for me.

I figured out that I did not have a passion for engineering. It was not for me. Even though I took calculus in high school, Calculus II kicked my butt! I was not cut out to be an engineer. I had no desire to stick with it.

Finally, it became obvious that I needed to learn more about God's Word. I was frustrated that I couldn't stand up to the sociology teacher. It bothered me that so many of my peers believed there was no hell and no God.

As I thought about what I wanted to do with my life, I remembered the times I played school and taught the kids at the church. Teaching was a natural fit. RPI was a great school for engineering, but to become an educator, I had to make a different choice. That's why after one year at RPI, I transferred to my dad's alma mater, Nyack Missionary College, now known as Nyack College. Fortunately, most of my credits transferred. I entered as a sophomore, still on target to graduate within the four years.

***

When fear is the driving force of our actions and behaviors, our lives become shame-filled, legalistic, and headed toward the dead-end pursuit of perfection. Living this way is as lonely as it is exhausting.

Life with Jesus, on the other hand, is a life filled with adventure, freedom, and wholeness. It's not about perfectionism, it's about relationship. The love of Jesus is free, no striving required.[1]

Campus life was different at Nyack. My course work consisted of everything I loved. I took education methods courses, psychology, and Bible.

Our dorms were segregated by gender, with the girls on the hill and the boys on the other side of the campus. I had the feeling that many of the students' parents sent them to the college in an attempt to keep them on the narrow path to heaven rather than the broad road to hell. In spite of all they did to try to keep us away from each other, I knew about more pregnancies on this campus than at RPI, a school three times the size of Nyack.

In the words of my mother, "People do what they want to do." If anything, the rules made it more appealing to the students. It was a challenge for the students to see how many times they could "cross the line" without getting caught.

I shared a room with two girls, Ellen from Pennsylvania and Lynn from New Jersey. Our room had a bunk bed and one single bed. We also had a common bathroom area again on the floor. My roommates were really sweet.

Lynn, whose parents were considerably older, lived in constant fear that she would get a call saying something happened to her parents. She explained that she was the surprise baby. Her mom thought she was going into menopause. Instead, she learned she was pregnant with Lynn. Now they were in their seventies.

My first year at Nyack, I built my schedule around *Days of Our Lives* and *General Hospital*. In fact, I remember getting so upset when the assassination attempt on President Reagan interrupted Luke and Laura's wedding! That's when I realized how much control these soap operas had on my life. I had more concern for these fictional characters than the health and well-being of the leader of our country. I knew I had to make a change.

My priorities were all wrong. I had to stop the daily diet of soap operas. It was impacting my thought processes and consuming too much of my energies.

I decided to major in elementary education with a minor in psychology. After my experience with my sociology teacher, I wanted to learn more about how people think. In addition to the regular core subjects for my program, I took Bible classes and attended chapel Monday through Friday. These services often featured keynote speakers. One guest in particular, Josh McDowell, author of *Why Wait*, was a frequent speaker.

"True love is spelled G-I-V-E. It is not based on what you can get but rooted in what you can give to the other person. Love can wait to give; it is lust that can't wait to get," McDonald would say. "Rules without relationship lead to rebellion."[2]

I viewed this statement through the lens of my relationship with Christ. Many in churches focused on the rules of engagement rather than on our need to be in a relationship with Christ. Without falling in love with Jesus, I would be prone to rebel against the principles he gave us in the Bible. So, it became a love thing for me.

My goal was to please my heavenly Father. I wanted to make him happy. Instead of viewing these rules as roadblocks that restricted me and kept me from having fun, I viewed them as guardrails. Like any good father, God put them in place to protect me from unnecessary heartache, sexual sin, disease, and unwanted pregnancies.

I appreciated Josh's "Why Wait" sermons. The messages made sense to me. They also reminded me of the commitment I made when I was sixteen to remain a virgin.

Chapter 15

CHANGE OF COURSE

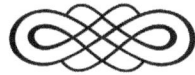

I finally made it to my last semester in college. It was 1983. In my college senior year, I worked part time in the computer library at IBM. The computer courses I took at RPI helped me secure the job.

It was the perfect gig. When I finished my tasks, they let me do my homework. My boss loved me and invited me to work with him again. He said there might even be a full-time job opening by the time I graduated that May.

Instead of living in the dorm, I moved back home my last semester at Nyack College. My student teaching assignment was in a neighboring district, and my house was closer to the elementary school. Besides, I only had one other class that met once a week. It did not make sense to pay for the extra room and board. I drove to the college on those days.

My first student teaching assignment was in the second grade. I loved working with the students. After that rotation, I moved to teaching sixth graders. I knew I had the potential to be a good teacher.

Teaching felt natural. I had a lot of fun with the students. More importantly, they learned the lessons I taught. But the adults were a different story. I was ill-equipped to deal with them. They do not teach you about the politics of education.

I was not welcomed into their "club." I hoped the only Black teacher in the entire building would take me under her wing. But she had no interest in helping me become successful. My host teachers were not much better. My student teaching experience soured me to the thought of a career in this field. So, I changed course.

I took my IBM manager up on the offer to work with him full time. So, the Monday after I graduated with my Bachelor of Science in Education from Nyack College, I started working third shift at IBM.

By the way, I did not get a car for this graduation either. My mother was a firm believer in the Lord blessing the child that gets her own. So, I borrowed one of my parents' cars and saved my money until I could afford to purchase my own car. By the next year, I had the down payment for a brand-new 1984 Honda Accord. I have to admit, it felt good knowing that I had gotten the car on my own.

I know, I know . . . How in the world did I get back into education? It was almost ten years before I returned. But keep reading, you will find out.

Chapter 16

HE TOOK MY TURN

Five years after graduating from college, I was still working at IBM. My dating life had not really taken off. I was still waiting for Mr. Right. But the pressure to find someone intensified when my younger brother, Brian, got married on October 3, 1988.

The day was hard. From the moment I got up, I had to face the reality that Brian was getting married before me. I was turning twenty-seven one week later on October 10. Brian was three years younger, yet he was experiencing a portion of life that I was still denied.

Before the ceremony, we gathered downstairs with my brother and several members of the wedding party. When Mom came out of the bathroom, her eyes met Brian's. As she looked at him, she said, "My son, the husband." That's when everyone started crying.

The wedding coordinator signaled that they were ready to start the ceremony. After the ushers escorted the mother of the bride and the mother of the groom to their seats, the processional began. Dad, in his role as pastor, performed the ceremony.

The wedding party, accommodating siblings, nieces, nephews, and close friends, was huge. Over three hundred people attended the wedding. All eyes were on us as we walked down the aisle. I was so glad I thought to grab some tissues before we started. I needed them.

Of course, I was happy for my brother, but I was also sad for me. I always imagined being the first to wed. I was the eldest grandchild on my dad's side and the fourth-oldest grandchild on my mother's. Sadly, that dream was not to be.

After the ceremony, we stayed behind to take pictures. By the time we were ready to head to the reception, it was pouring rain. In my mind, the clouds were shedding tears for me.

I'm not sure how the three hundred plus guests crammed into the reception hall, but they did. After my brother and his new bride cut their cake, I walked around to greet the family and friends who were there. That's when one of the women stopped me to ask me a question.

"So, when are we going to have some cake?"

"Excuse me?" I asked.

"You know. When are we going to get a piece of that wedding cake?"

"I am sure the waiters will bring it out as soon as they finish cutting it," I said.

"No, your cake?"

My cake? I just looked at her, not sure how, or even whether to respond to such an asinine question. Did she think she was being cute? She spoke to me as if I had control over if and when I would get married.

I can't believe she had the audacity to ask me that question in the middle of my brother's wedding reception. I felt like she was taunting me. It was another dagger in my already aching heart.

Perhaps she meant well, but it was the last question I wanted to hear. I had my own question. *When Lord? When?* But no answers came that day.

***

A week after my brother and his wife returned from their honeymoon, we gathered to look at their wedding video. My mother entered the room after we started playing the video and asked us to rewind it to the beginning. We explained to her that it was the beginning. She looked at us and then back at the screen.

Rather than hiring a professional, a friend had videotaped the ceremony. This was a mistake. We missed a lot of moments that we could never get back. After that experience, I decided I would make sure that did not happen to anyone else in our family. This started my passion for videography.

I did not realize it at the time, but my camcorder provided a side benefit. Now when I showed up to events, I wasn't alone. My camera was my partner. I captured the moments while my "companion" shielded me. With my lens in hand, I became the interviewer rather than the interviewee. I was present, yet not there.

Chapter 17

SHE'S THIRSTY

I often think about how God must sit back and just laugh at me as I tell him what I'm going to do and what I'm not going to do. Like the all-knowing parent, I can hear him say, *Let's watch her. This will be amusing.*

He chuckles as I continue to run through the maze looking for cheese that he's moved. Instead of learning from my mistakes, I kept running into the same dead-end walls. That's how I describe my dating experience in my late twenties, thirties, and early forties.

My increasing age, combined with my family and friends getting married before me, ignited a match in my self-serving relationship efforts. Almost every single Black man I came into contact with was a potential mate. No, I did not go to bars or clubs, but I did frequent church services and gospel concerts. I convinced myself that I had to be where the boys were. My actions did not go unnoticed. The comments the onlookers made got back to me:

"Watch out for her. She's THIRSTY."

"What do you mean?" a potential candidate asked.

"Paula is shopping for a man. That girl is so desperate for a man that she **T**hrows **H**erself **I**nto **R**elationships, **S**ticking **T**o **Y**ou."

The woman's comments were true, but I couldn't help it. I fell into a fruitless cycle of girl chasing boy, boy slowing down, boy getting caught—only to find out he was caught by someone else. It happened over and over again. All I had to do was insert the new guy's name. Today, as I flip through the pages of my journal, the pattern is obvious. I fell into "love" as quickly as the changing seasons.

> Oct 04, 1992: Dear Lord, I really don't know what you're doing with this friendship. I do know I'm growing in love with BAK.
>
> Oct 10, 1998: The first person to wish me happy birthday today was B. God, he is so sweet! For the first time I verbalized that I'm growing in love with him! Boy, that was the hardest thing I've had to do in quite a while. It's a scary feeling! I really believe he is growing in love with me too."
>
> May 20, 2009: From the day I laid eyes on you in PA at the training, I felt a connection with you.
>
> Aug 10, 2009: Viva Las Vegas!!! I'm here with Aunt Shelby. It's been a great combo of rest, relaxation, and recreation. The trip here was uneventful. My deepest

longing was that you would show up at the airport ready to fly to Vegas with me!

Nov 09, 2009: I long to hear from you, but I cope with the temptation of calling by writing in this book.

Jan 24, 2010: The challenge for me is trusting God to instill in him a love for me. Although I'd love to be here with him, it's not what I expect. I'm willing to follow him wherever he goes.

There were countless entries just like this. I would find a guy that I liked, chase them, and hope and pray that they would reciprocate the feelings. Needless to say, this did not work for me.

***

Around 1989, there was a guy I worked with at IBM who would hang out in my office. He was not a Christian. He didn't even go to church. I knew I should not entertain the idea of dating him, but I did not care. Although we didn't have sex, we did a lot of kissing. I began sneaking around to meet him. I used my younger siblings as a cover.

Word to the wise: Don't do that! First of all, because I was emotionally wrapped up with the guy, he got me to "loan" him $5000 for a business venture. *Stupid!* Second, my siblings ratted me out.

I still lived in the basement of my parents' house. One Saturday evening, I drove my siblings, Ann and Alan, my baby brother, to the Galleria Mall. After my rendezvous at the mall with the guy, my siblings told my parents. My folks waited until I was asleep, then came to my room. It was a sneak attack.

"You're grown. You can date who you want to date. But if you are going to do wrong, leave our children out of it," my dad said. "That goes for the kids at the church too."

Right there, he forbade me to do any ministry at the church. I couldn't sing, work with the youth program, or teach Sunday school.

How dare they rat me out, I thought. I was ticked off. I was more upset about my siblings tattling on me than being convicted that being "unequally yoked" violated God's plan for my life.

The next morning, rather than drive to the church. I drove to a nearby park. I sat in my car and wept. The look of disappointment on my dad's face convicted me. Just as I had hurt my parents, I knew the Lord was even more disappointed in my decisions. After all, God knew the whole story.

Prior to the start of the morning service, with tears in my eyes, I went to my dad's office and asked for his forgiveness. During service, the Lord continued to speak to me. I asked for the Lord to forgive me and give me the strength to only date those who were prequalified. In other words, they will minimally need to be in a relationship with Jesus.

Like the placement of guardrails on the road, I realized the Lord desired to protect me and my relationship with him. Everything I needed for a successful relationship, I could find in his Word. If I had listened to "Be ye not unequally yoked together with unbelievers: for what fellowship hath righteousness with unrighteousness? and what communion hath light with darkness?" (2 Corinthians 6:14 KJV), I would have avoided the scene with my parents, saved $5000, and been spared the humiliation of being sat down in front of the entire church.

That morning, before my father preached his sermon, he made the entire choir sit in the audience. He realized, if my siblings knew, others in the choir had to be complicit in the relationship too. He reminded all of us of our responsibility to hold each other accountable for living out our faith. "What shall we say then? Shall we continue in sin that grace may abound? Certainly not! How shall we who died to sin live any longer in it?" (Romans 6:1–2 KJV).

This was a pivotal moment in my life. I learned my lesson. But most importantly, I realized if my relationship had to be a covert operation, I probably *should not have been* in the relationship!

Afterward, I started becoming the best version of myself. Rather than obsessing about finding a man, I realized that I did not need a man in order to live a fulfilled life.

Chapter 18

HE DOESN'T DESERVE YOU

O nce I realized I didn't *need* a man, my attitude changed. I began to believe that I was the prize. This allowed me to raise my standards and what I would accept from a man.

I continued working at IBM. It was now 1990. I was 29.

"'For I know the plans I have for you,' declares the Lord, 'plans to prosper you and not to harm you, plans to give you a hope and a future'" (Jeremiah 29:11). That was the Scripture in the devotion I read that day. I did not recall seeing this verse before. But if I did, it certainly never resonated with me like it did that day.

The words leaped off the page and into my heart. I needed those words. They reassured me that, regardless of what was going on, God was with me, and he had a specific plan for my life.

***

My father always told me the man that deserved me would take the time to learn who I was. He said they would appreciate me, with all my flaws. Dad had a simple test. I still remember when he used it for the first time with Thomas, one of the men I dated.

Thomas came over to the house and started talking with my dad.

"Pastor Palmer, I love your daughter."

My father's lip and eyebrow turned up. "Love her. You don't even know her!"

"Why would you say that, sir?"

"Okay. I'll give you the benefit of the doubt, but let me ask you a question," Dad said. "What is Paula's middle name?"

Thomas looked at me and then back at my father with empty eyes. He had no idea what my full name was, and my father knew it.

"Like I said, you don't even know her. You're not in love with her; at best, you are in lust with her."

I didn't want to admit it, but I knew my father was right. Thomas and I met at IBM. We spent a great deal of time together, riding to and from work. We saw each other at church too. Our conversations never amounted to anything of great depth.

I'm not sure if I just liked the idea of having someone to do things with, or if I was really into him. One thing I did know, something about him did not make sense.

Thomas's family was Panamanian. When I flew south to Florida to spend time with Thomas and his family, I was uncomfortable with what I heard and saw.

When we got to the house, his mom was very cordial. She offered me food and allowed me to pick fresh oranges off the trees in their backyard. Mrs. Jimenez was a dark, round, short woman, with a few missing teeth.

Once Thomas's dad got home, she kept her head down and stopped speaking. His presence filled the room. His blue jeans were held up by suspenders. Mr. Jimenez's bulging stomach hung over his pants.

He threw his straw hat on the table, then glared at his wife. She appeared to make herself even smaller.

"Hey Dad. This is my girlfriend, Paula. We met on the job."

Mr. Jimenez turned and looked at me.

"It's nice to meet you, Mr. Jimenez."

Mr. Jimenez nodded without a word to me, but instead said something in Spanish to Thomas.

"Come on, Paula, let's go sit in the sunroom."

"What was that about?" I asked.

"Nothing," he said. But the look on Thomas's face made me think there was a lot more to the story.

That evening, Thomas stayed at his brother's for the evening.

In the wee hours of the morning, I woke up to Mr. Jimenez yelling at his wife, partly in Spanish and English. Although I was in a room on the opposite end of the house, I still heard them. The sound permeated the walls.

The obscenities were clear, but it was hard to interpret what else he said because it was a mixture of Spanish and English. However, what scared me was hearing a loud thud and then Mrs. Jimenez's cries. With each sound, I prayed that we would all make it through the night.

***

A couple of weeks after Thomas and I returned from visiting his parents, he purchased a home. He asked me to come over and help him move in. I brought my youngest brother, Alan, with me.

"Paula, your phone is ringing," Alan said.

My phone was in my pocketbook in the room where Alan was watching TV.

"Would you get my phone and bring it to me, please."

After I conversed on the phone a few minutes, Thomas immediately began asking me questions.

"Who was that?" Thomas asked.

"A friend."

"A male friend?"

"What difference does it make?"

This angered Thomas. He raised his hand to strike me.

"Negro, have you *lost your mind?*"

I blurted out the words almost as quickly as he raised his hand. I may not have realized it before, but I was clear now.

Thomas was not for me. I could not believe what I just witnessed . . . but yes, I could.

After visiting with his mother and father and hearing the abuse, I should have known that it was in Thomas. One cannot be a part of trauma like that without it affecting them. Either they run from it, or they internalize and repeat the behavior.

Thomas evidently became what he saw. The difference was I was not going to take it. I was not willing to be a part of the pattern.

So when he raised his hand, he closed his chance of a future with me. Now I was back to a familiar place—uncoupled again.

After this breakup, I turned to others for advice. I wanted to learn from their experience. Michelle McKinney Hammond was one author who had several books on being a Christian single. I purchased several of them. I was desperate to learn the lessons so I could pass the test.

Chapter 19

GETTING BACK ON TRACK

After the relationship with Thomas, I stopped trying to be coupled, and instead focused on developing myself and others. Even though I went to work for IBM right after graduation, I still loved working with children. I invested a lot of my time and energy into helping them.

My boss at IBM allowed me to take my lunch break at the end of the day so I could provide homework help and tutoring to the students. In 1988, this led to the development of the Multi-Service Center, my not-for-profit organization, and the start of the King's Kids community program, a free weekly program where we serviced children ages four-to-eighteen-years.

I ran the program for a couple of years at my old elementary school. I would use the church van to pick up students from other schools to bring them to my program. Many of the students really needed our help. I could also see that there were students who were not being challenged enough by their teachers. This frustrated me since I was able to get these same students to work at high levels.

Twice a year, we would do full dramatic productions. The same kids that the teachers said needed to be in special education memorized multiple pages of script and played instruments. These same students entertained and commanded the audience's attention. This became the topic of conversation at our extended family's Thanksgiving Dinner. We gathered at Grandma Nellie's house.

It was November 1991. While sitting at the dinner table, I brought up the topic of teachers and the poor job they were doing with many of our children, especially the Black ones. At the time Aunt Zola, my father's youngest sister, was on the school board.

As I continued to complain about our school system, Aunt Zola put the palm of her hand in my face. "I don't want to hear it. You're sitting at IBM with a teaching degree when you could be a part of the solution. Until you're ready to do something about it, this conversation is over!"

Wow. I was not expecting that reaction. However, Aunt Zola had a point. When I first graduated, I was not ready to deal with the politics of teaching. But now I knew I could take on the challenge. Aunt Zola was the catalyst for me reversing course and getting back on track with my teaching career.

Over that holiday season, I spoke with my manager at IBM and arranged to work from home. Unlike today, this was a novelty in the 1990s. I needed a separate landline to use with my new dial-up modem. That's how I connected to the computers at my job. By January 1992, I was ready to act. I started subbing, applied to the master's degree program at New Paltz College, and started looking for a job.

In July 1992, I was hired to teach at the elementary school I had attended, John F. Kennedy. I would return and be the type of teacher that I wanted as a child. I knew one thing; I would not be like Ms. Cratchet. I can still recall an incident that happened with her when I was four.

"Would you open this for me?" I reached up to place the box in her large brown hand. I tried to open it, but I couldn't. My little hands did not have the dexterity to open the milk carton.

"Are you stupid or something!"

I quivered as I fought back the pool of tears forming in the corners of my big brown eyes. Those cutting words came from my kindergarten teacher. I asked her to help me open my milk carton, and that was her retort.

How could I know what to do with this strange box? That's not the kind of milk the man delivered to our house. Our milk came in bottles, not cardboard boxes.

But the damage was done; her words stuck in my head. I shook my head no, while inside I screamed, *I'll show you!*

Now, I was prepared to return to the place of my injury, decades later, to protect other little children from teachers like Ms. Cratchet.

I immediately turned in my letter of resignation to my manager. It was perfect timing. IBM was in the process of downsizing, and I was able to take advantage of the opportunity.

They offered me a substantial severance package. This money paid for my master's courses. Even though becoming a teacher would result in a pay cut, I did not care. Nothing could curb my excitement. It was a full circle moment. That's how I entered the teaching field.

During my waiting period for a mate, I invested in myself. I continued adding to my academic credentials. My parents always encouraged me to want more. In fact, at the graduation when I earned my administrative certification, my dad celebrated the moment, but in the same breath said, "Wait until you get your doctorate." His words stayed in my head.

I originally started working on my doctorate at Columbia University while I was still a teacher. When it came time to matriculate into a specific doctoral program, I was denied entry. The timing was not right.

So, throughout the 1990s, I also used the time to invest in the children's lives. Some of my favorite times were when the girls slept over our house. We would have upward of fifteen teenagers there at one time. All of us, in our footy pajamas, would sit around laughing and talking. We would bring our blankets and sleeping bags to the back deck, where we watched the latest movie on a portable screen. It was like our own private drive-in theater. Whether it was *Parent Trap, High School Musical,* or *The Thief in the Night* movie that had impacted my childhood so deeply, this was a part of our tradition.

Part of the fun was staying up all night. Woe to those that dared to fall asleep. They were met with toothpaste in their hand, then a feather or tickle on their face.

The night was not complete until we made our trip to the local Walmart in our pajamas at about four in the morning. We always had a wonderful time making memories.

I used those times to talk to the girls about sex. I encouraged them to remain virgins until they got married. They were real discussions. The girls always wanted to know how far they could go.

I'm sure every generation struggles with this question. The older I get, the more I realize the danger in this approach to sex. I am astutely aware that Satan wants to destroy our lives. Jesus said, "The thief cometh not, but for to steal, and to kill, and to destroy: I am come that they might have life, and that they might have it more abundantly" (John 10:10). My journey has shown me that if the enemy can keep us from fulfilling the purpose for which we were created, in a way, it is a win for him. The guilt that accompanies the first time one has sex outside of marriage, an unexpected pregnancy, or a sexually transmitted disease, and the broken relationship that results from an infidelity are all examples of how we can impact our futures. However, I find hope in the words of the second portion of Jesus's words. I believe if we follow the principles found in the Bible, we will have an abundant, purpose driven life.

It is hard to explain how satisfying it was to reignite this part of my life. It was fulfilling to know that I was having an impact on hundreds of children. In some way, by helping them and their families, it satisfied a need in my own life. I often referred to myself as the "mother of none, yet mother of all." My singlehood season afforded me the time and joy of shaping the lives of these children without the 24/7 responsibility of caring for them. It was a win-win!

Chapter 20

YOU'VE GOT MAIL

My romantic life followed a distinct pattern. June often marked momentous occasions in my life. The summer of 1996 was no different.

I realized people communicate more through their actions than by what they say. They tend to show you exactly who they are. The question is what we will do with this information once we have it. I faced this decision with my latest beau, Devin. We were experiencing our fairy tale in real life.

The dial-up modem seemed to take forever. I could hear the different tones as it tried to connect me to the rest of the world. When I opened my AOL account, I heard, "You've Got Mail."

Somehow, my email address showed up on a distribution list regarding the upcoming Auxiliaries in Ministry Conference in Indianapolis, Indiana. This was a popular conference in our church organization. Each year the conference moved from city to city across the states. But this year, I opted to attend the Camp Meeting in Columbus, Ohio instead.

The email read, "Saints, let's pray for the success of our conference." Without thinking, I responded that I would pray for the conference but would not attend because I had other plans. Then I sent the email off. Its recipient was Devin Bradford.

To my surprise, Devin responded to my email. He asked me a few general questions, and I replied. We volleyed back and forth with our email responses. By the fourth email, he asked if my husband was going with me to the Camp Meeting. I informed him I was not married.

He responded by asking me for my number. I did not expect that request. However, I gladly obliged. He called. I picked up the phone so quickly the cord nearly knocked my phone to the floor.

My stomach did flip-flops as I answered the phone. On the other end was a warm, inviting baritone voice. His southwestern drawl made me swoon. That first day we talked for hours.

I learned that he lived in a small town in Oklahoma, and he was planning to drive people from his dad's church to Indianapolis for Auxiliaries in Ministry (AIM). Devin was also a preacher's kid. Both of our mothers were missionaries in our church. We were also both teachers. He taught science at the junior high school level. His school was already out on their summer break. I still had a few more days left in the school year.

A few days later, Devin called with a proposition.

"Columbus is only 175 miles from where I'll be in Indianapolis. I'd love to see you in person."

My mind was racing now. We had talked every day for a week, but I had no idea what he looked like. Was it possible? Would I finally see him in the flesh? (This was before the advent of cell phones with video cameras.)

After Devin got approval from my father, we planned to meet on that Saturday at Cracker Barrel in Columbus, Ohio. I told him I would be wearing a yellow shirt and jeans.

My father allowed me to borrow his portable car phone. The case weighed about five pounds. Even though I was thirty-five years old, it was the first time I would be driving that far away by myself. The ride from my house was over eight hours. I felt safer having the car phone with me.

Chapter 21

THE MEETING

Devin and I met for brunch at Cracker Barrel. He arrived before I did, so, when I walked into the store section of the restaurant, he noticed me first.

I wore my jeans and yellow shirt so he could spot me. My hair was twisted in a French bun. Shortly after I walked into the store, he got up and headed in my direction.

He looked nothing like I imagined. His smile made me feel safe. Devin was fair-skinned, with a mustache and a medium build. He was a foot taller than me.

I instantly felt a connection with him. After we ate, we spent some time at a nearby park. As usual, I brought my camera and a blanket too. When it was time for him to leave, I didn't want to see him go.

"Why don't you follow me back to Indianapolis? I'll get you a room."

After calling and checking in with my parents, that's exactly what I did.

By the time we arrived in Indianapolis, it was almost time for the evening service. As promised, Devin purchased my hotel room. He followed me to the room carrying my bags. Once safely in the room, he told me he was going back to his room to get changed, and he would pick me up in twenty-five minutes.

Since it was a national church conference, I actually knew a lot of people there. Several people drove from the Northeast to attend. I think that also added to my comfort level. There were at least thirty people I could call on if I needed them.

Devin and I had an incredible time in Indianapolis. We took time away from the conference to get to know one another. He took me to the zoo on one day and the aquarium on another. We even visited with one of my mom's nursing friends. I had not seen her since I was a little girl.

That Thursday was the Fourth of July. Devin decided to drive us to Cincinnati so he could introduce me to his only sibling. When we arrived at her place, I stuck out my hand for her to shake it. Instead, she grabbed me and gave me a great big hug. It all felt very natural.

Devin explained to her how we had met via email about ten days before and how he convinced me to go to Indianapolis. We talked with her for hours. The night was capped off with spectacular fireworks in and outside the car! My emotions were heightened. *Is he the one? This has to be God.*

The week was magical. After leaving the conference, instead of driving home, I drove to Aunt Shelby's house in Gaithersburg, Maryland. Devin and I talked on our car phones most of the nine-and-a-half-hour drive there.

***

Now, less than a month later, Devin was meeting my immediate family and most of my extended ones too. He flew into New York to attend a function with me. Our church was hosting a banquet at The Capri 400 banquet hall in Port Ewen.

Devin wore a black suit, and I wore a black gown. It felt good to show up at the banquet with someone. This was the first time in a long time that I did not have to go alone, or with my camera. Several of my extended family members were in town for the event.

After the banquet, while we were back at my parents' house, Dad invited Devin to preach at the Sunday service the next day. This was a great sign of Dad's approval. I was giddy to have him speak and for everyone to see I was dating a minister. The congregation enjoyed him.

Since it was August, and school didn't start for a couple more weeks, I decided to fly back to Oklahoma with Devin. Our relationship advanced quickly. Even though we lived over a thousand miles apart, we managed to see each other a couple of times every month. Devin stayed with my brother Brian and his family when he came to see me. When I went to Oklahoma, I stayed with a friend of his family.

By the end of August, we were talking about getting married. Devin started introducing me as his fiancée even though I did not have a ring. He wanted the women in his sphere to know he was taken. We began making wedding plans.

We decided to get married the following June after school finished. We would have the entire summer to honeymoon and get settled. "Can I be in your wedding?" became one of the most frequently asked questions that fall. People in my church knew my journey.

I was thirty-five years old. They knew I trusted God in my season of singleness, and they rejoiced with me that the season was ending. With all of my siblings and friends, my wedding party jumped to seven couples plus the ring bearer and flower girl.

Mom and Dad liked Devin. They attempted to establish a relationship with his parents too. They knew the importance of having supportive in-laws, especially since I would be moving near Devin's family. They wanted to help nurture that relationship.

Mrs. Jean Bradford, Devin's mom, was an interesting character. I called her Mother Jean. The first time I met her, she berated all of Devin's ex-girlfriends. "That girl was a hoochie momma. You should see the way she dressed," said Mother Jean.

"Mother Jean, we are going to have a problem if you talk about me to your friends the way you are talking about Devin's ex-girlfriends." The words came out of my mouth before I could stop them. I was usually never that direct. But her words rubbed me the wrong way. I could not believe a good Christian missionary and pastor's wife was so toxic.

She looked at me with her squinted eyes.

"So, I hear New York women are fast," she said.

"What do you mean by that?" I asked.

"You know. They sleep around."

"Well, I cannot speak for all the women in New York, but that is not my story," I said.

"How old are you?" she asked.

"Thirty-five."

"Hmm," she grunted, then rolled her eyes. Devin was three years younger than me.

"I am a virgin." I looked at my watch. *Where is Devin?* I thought. Devin had a side job at Walmart. So I was left alone with his mother. *He should be getting home soon*, I thought.

"My son is going to be a pastor. He needs a woman that can support his ministry."

"Mother Jean, I'm a preacher's kid. I know this life very well."

"Yes, but do you know Oklahoma? We have expectations."

Thank God, Devin is back. I could hear him parking the car in the driveway. I ran to the door to let him in. "Don't you ever leave me alone with her again," I whispered.

"Why? What's wrong?" he asked.

"I'll tell you later."

After putting away the items he purchased from the store, Devin and I left the house.

That was my introduction to Devin's mother. Based on my experience, I wasn't sure how a meeting with my parents would go.

That November, both sets of parents were attending the national church convocation in Memphis, Tennessee. My parents suggested to Devin's parents that they meet in person while they were in Memphis. My parents' invitation was met with reluctance by Devin's. However, they agreed to meet one another at the conference.

"I thought we would at least go out for coffee," my mother told me after they met. The entire exchange lasted about five minutes. After the initial introductions, Devin's mother did all the talking. Her husband didn't say anything. Then they left.

"I think she felt intimidated," my mother said. "You know how we dress when we are at these church services." My mother had her fancy hat, sequined dress, and color-coordinated accessories. That's not how Mother Jean dressed. The economic disparity between the two couples was glaring. "I think she was self-conscious about the way they looked," Mom said.

Well, that certainly didn't help Mother Jean feel any more comfortable about Devin and me.

***

We survived the parents' meeting. It was now a week before Christmas. I was back in Oklahoma.

It was strange seeing Christmas decorations when it was eighty degrees outside. There was something about seeing signs of Christmas when it was beach weather rather than ski weather. It was foreign to me. The ornaments looked out of place.

Devin and I were leaving to go to the airport the next day on Christmas. The engagement party would be on New Year's Eve.

We still had a lot to do. We also needed to settle some things, like where we would live.

"So, my parents offered to let us move into their trailer."

"Excuse me?"

"We can move in with my parents when you come down here."

"Devin, I am not living here in your mother's house. I'm sure we can find a reasonable apartment until we are ready to purchase a home." Devin had no answer to my reaction. He just continued driving the car.

"Where are we going?" I asked.

"To the mall." Devin and I only had a few more hours in Oklahoma. I still did not have my ring, and the engagement party was in a few days. I wondered when he was going to officially propose.

It was as if Devin read my mind. When we got to the mall, we walked into Helzberg Diamonds. I never allowed myself to go into a jewelry store and window shop for rings before. All those sparkling diamonds. It was like a scene out of the movie, *Sweet Home Alabama.*

"Paula, come look at these," Devin said. "Which one do you like?"

I pointed to a gold solitaire round-cut diamond ring. The jeweler took the ring out of the case and put it on my finger.

"We'll take that one," Devin said.

Oh, my goodness. This was the time, I thought.

"Paula, let me hold your credit card."

Wait! What did he ask me for? Did I hear him correctly?

My face must have shown my confusion because he followed up by saying, "Don't worry, I just need your information to finalize the sale. I will pay the bill. My mom has access to my bank account, so I can't get to my money now."

What? That made no sense! I thought.

But I dutifully handed Devin my credit card and ignored the alarms going off in my head. The trade-off for my silence was a beautiful diamond ring.

It will all work out. I tried to reassure myself that Devin would keep his end of the bargain. *Besides, it will be our secret. No one needs to know.*

Although it was not the grand gesture that I envisioned, I rationalized that at least I had a ring on my finger. As we drove back to the house, I looked at the ring. It was beautiful. Now the engagement felt official. Even though I kept holding my hand in a position so his parents would notice the ring, they never did.

"Devin, this is our last Christmas Eve before we get married. Why don't we take your parents out tonight."

"I do not think that is a good idea, Paula."

"Why not?" I asked.

"Just trust me."

Forever the optimist, I pushed him into it. "I think we should spend some time with them. A dinner would be nice. We are flying to New York early in the morning. Maybe this will make up for you missing Christmas Day."

It was strange to me that even though the engagement party was a week away, Devin still did not know if any of his groomsmen or family members were coming. He never shared the drama that went on behind the scenes. That alone should have set off additional alarms about our relationship, but I ignored them because I wanted the fairy-tale ending.

The wedding plans were going well. We ordered the bridesmaid dresses and my gown. My first fitting was scheduled for after the holidays. We already put a down payment on the honeymoon, and the restaurant was reserved for the reception. The only thing we needed to do was order the wedding announcements and put the engagement picture in our local papers. We would do that after the party.

"Okay," Devin said. "I will invite them out to dinner with us."

Devin packed a suitcase. Mine was already in the trunk of the car. We stayed in front of the TV while Devin's parents remained in their bedroom until it was time to leave for dinner.

"I don't know why you two keep talking about getting married. I ain't seen no ring. You need to stop talking until you have one," Mother Jean said.

Devin's parents sat in the backseat of the car. When she finished her statement, I raised my ring finger to show her.

"I cannot believe you, Devin. You gave her a ring without showing it to me first! How did you buy it?"

Devin and his father said nothing. I followed the men's lead and remained silent until we arrived at the restaurant.

After the waitress showed us to our table, we sat and looked at the menu. Mother Jean sat directly in front of me. Devin was to my right and his father to my left. After the waitress brought the food to the table, Devin's mother proceeded to let me know how she felt.

"That's it. I can't take this anymore." Mother Jean slammed her fork on the table. "You are not the one for my son."

With each word her voice grew louder. The waitress approached the table to ask if we needed anything but quickly turned and walked away. I felt like the eyes of everyone around us were now focused on our table.

I looked at Devin, then his father. The two of them locked their eyes on their plates and kept eating. I kicked Devin's foot under the table. Nothing.

"You need to go back to wherever you came from and leave my son alone."

I could feel my body temperature rise. I just looked at her. The mother of the man I was marrying, this Christian missionary woman, this woman who preached Jesus, but obviously did not know what it meant to live like Jesus, was publicly humiliating me. I wanted to disappear under the table.

I motioned for the waitress. "May we have the check, please."

The men were still eating their food. It was as if they went dumb and blind. They acted as if this was a normal dinner. I barely touched my food. The waitress put it in a to-go container for me. After paying for the meal, I got up and quickly walked to the car. The silence was as thick as the darkness.

No one said a word as we took Devin's parents back to their trailer. But as soon as they left the car, I started in on Devin. "Would you please tell me when the 'leave and cleave' part of this relationship is going to begin?" The Bible speaks of the man leaving his father and mother to start a new family unit with his bride. Devin seemed to be having a big problem doing this.

"Paula, you do not understand."

"Do you know how embarrassing that was for me? I'm your responsibility. Why didn't you come to my rescue?"

Devin never sufficiently answered my question. This haunted me for weeks. The doubts were rushing back into my mind.

We had passed through four of the five Christian dating stages: prospecting, connecting, qualifying, and coupling, and I had ample data. Now that we were formally entering the commitment stage, I had to figure out what I was going to do with it.

***

We flew back to New York and celebrated Christmas with my family. Devin kept leaving the room to talk on the phone.

"What's going on?" I asked.

"They are not coming."

"Who is not coming?

"All of them, my parents, my sister, my groomsmen. None of them are coming."

"What? Don't they realize how important this is for us?"

Devin shrugged his shoulders. In the days leading up to the engagement party, Devin kept calling his family and friends, hoping they would change their minds. They did not.

The day of the party, Devin took back my ring before my family and friends converged on our house. Before we sat down to eat, we formed a circle in the middle of our living room. Dad prayed over our relationship and the food. Before we moved into the dining room, Devin got on his knees in front of everyone and formally asked me to marry him. Everyone oohed and aahed at the sight of my ring. Once we sat around the dining room table, Devin recounted our romance. It was the first time I heard the whole story from his perspective. It felt great listening to him talk about the way my voice made him feel when we started talking on the phone. And what he thought when he first saw me at Cracker Barrel. His memories filled me with hope.

The evening was wonderful, but a tinge of sadness rested over the festivities. Devin was hurt that no one was there to support him.

Chapter 22

BROKEN DREAMS

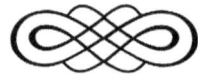

O nce Devin left on January 1, we continued with our daily calls. I started sending my books and other items to his house that I no longer needed to keep in my classroom. I also packed and sent some of my summer clothes.

Devin asked me to come back to Oklahoma for his bishop's banquet at the end of the month. Devin was one of his assistants, and he wanted me to meet him. I purchased a black sequined gown for the event. But in the back of my mind, a flurry of doubts continued to float around, clouding my thoughts about our relationship.

As I prepared to return to Oklahoma, I couldn't shake the feelings about his mother. My relationship with Mother Jean was still chilly. When I went to the house, after saying hello, we had little else to share. I never had a problem with parents liking me, so this whole scenario was foreign to me.

The banquet was that evening. Devin drove me to the venue. He introduced me to some people from his church, and to his bishop. After that, Devin was preoccupied with tasks related to the banquet, so much of the evening I sat alone in a corner.

Is this a glimpse into our future?

I flew back to New York on Sunday morning. That evening, I had a hard time sleeping. I dreamed about how life would be after we got married. It was my subconscious raising the red flag and waving it in front of my face.

In the dream, Devin and I got into a heated argument. In the middle of the argument, he left the house. "Great . . . run back to your mommy!"

I woke up with sweat on my face. My heart was beating fast.

In the stillness of the night, a light came on in my mind. *I can't do this!* The thought terrified me. The wedding plans were already in full motion. The girls had already paid for their gowns. I did a fitting, and they altered my dress, so they would not take it back. This whole thing was a nightmare. But deep down, I knew I could not go through with the wedding.

After work, as usual, Devin called me once he got home from work.

"Hey, Babe."

"Hi, Devin."

"Are you okay? You don't sound like yourself."

"No, I'm not."

"What's wrong?"

"Devin, I had a horrible dream! It scared me."

"What was it about?"

"You! You chose your mother over me. I cannot marry you without a guarantee that you have my back. So far, your behavior hasn't shown me that you love me more than your mother. I can't do this, Devin. The wedding is off!"

I did not wait for a reply. I hung up the phone. That act released a flow of tears that I could not stop.

I slowly walked up the stairs to speak with my parents.

"What's wrong?" my mother asked.

"The wedding is off!"

"What!" my dad answered.

"Oh, Paula. Are you sure?" Mom asked. She could see the pain in my face.

"Yes."

Mom wrapped her arms around me and squeezed me like only a loving mother could. That made me cry harder.

"Now I have to tell everyone."

"Why don't you wait until service on Sunday. You can tell everyone at the same time. You never know, maybe things will change."

"He's not going to change," I said.

The week dragged on. Each day, I hoped Devin would call and fight for me. I wanted him to say he would move to New York. I wanted him to stand up to his mother, but it never happened.

Chapter 23

GAIN THROUGH THE PAIN

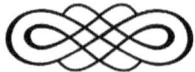

I t was the worst heartache I ever experienced. I cried for months. Although I would never harm myself, I could understand how people commit suicide. You just want the pain to stop. I could not even walk into a Walmart because it reminded me of Devin.

I sent the ring back to Helzberg Diamonds. I felt stupid. I called Devin and asked him to return my things. He never did return my stuff. It was so painful.

During my grieving season, my mom was tuned into my emotions. Without fail, when I walked up the stairs in the wee hours of the morning, my mother was there with her arms outstretched to wrap me in her love and concern. Dad, on the other hand, not so much. It was a completely different story.

I remember sitting in the living room crying with my mother in the early morning hours. It was still dark outside. My father got out of bed to find out where my mother had gone. When he saw us hugging on the couch, he said, "Oh," then turned around to head back to their bedroom.

"You're not going to stay and cry with us?" I asked.

The expression on my father's face was priceless. It was the comic relief we needed. As he went back to his bedroom, my mother and I started laughing.

***

That Sunday, at the end of the service, my father allowed me to have comments. I looked out in the audience and saw my "work mom." Aline was one of the staff members from my school. But more importantly, she was a sister in Christ. I told her about the broken engagement, and she said she would come to our church service to provide me emotional support as I made the announcement to my church family. It was good seeing her smiling face. As I stood up to talk, I locked my eyes on hers.

"I want to thank you all for your excitement, love, and support during our engagement period. But the wedding is off. Please don't ask." With my announcement, there was an audible gasp from the crowd. I saw some of the women wiping their eyes. After I made my announcement, I quickly sat down. I did not want to break down in front of all those people.

After that experience, it seemed like every woman I came in contact with had a horrible engagement story of their own. The one that shocked me the most was from my father's mother, Grandma Nellie. She lived around the corner from the school where I taught, so I often stopped by the house to see her. I was crying when I walked into Grandma Nellie's house. I had everything I could do to keep myself together in front of my first-grade class. There were a couple of times when I had to ask someone to supervise my class so I could pull myself together.

Grandma Nellie gave me a hug. "Paula, I know how you feel. I had a similar thing happen to me, twice. But each time, I was actually at the church getting ready to get married."

"What? What happened? Who were the guys?"

"Your uncle Jeremy's father, Bernard, was the first guy that jilted me. I told him I was pregnant, and he said we would get married. I was eighteen. We planned the wedding for October 19, 1940. Jeremy was eight months old, and your dad was two.

"The day of the wedding, I was at the church getting dressed. Suddenly, someone came in and said, 'Bernard is not coming.' That joker enlisted in the army on October 16 and was on his way to training camp. I was devastated, embarrassed, and hurt."

"Grandma Nellie, I never knew that!"

"Oh, you haven't heard it all yet. After I finally got myself back together, I started dating Fitz. That's when I got pregnant with your Aunt Laila. We were supposed to get married on June 21, 1941. I was three months pregnant with her. Would you believe Fitz did the same exact thing that Bernard did? The Wednesday before we were supposed to get married, he enlisted in the army too. Then he jumped on a bus and got out of town. I didn't find out until I was at the church waiting for the ceremony to begin."

The conversation with my grandmother was enlightening and comforting at the same time. I wasn't the only one who suffered the public humiliation of a broken engagement. At least I could hold my head up high because it was my decision.

The next couple of months held a number of difficult days for me. David Bridal kept calling me to come and pick up my dress. I couldn't bring myself to go get it. When I finally got up the nerve to retrieve the dress, I cried on the way there and back. At one point, I was crying so hard I couldn't see the road. I had to pull the car over.

That's when Donnie McClurkin's song, "Stand" came on the radio. I felt God's love envelop me. He was giving me the answer to the question, "How can you smile while your heart has been broken and filled with pain?" That song reminded me that I would be okay. I would get through this. All I knew was I wanted the pain to go away.

The next morning, as I drove to work, I cried all the way. As I turned onto the highway, suddenly the flashing lights of a police car were visible in my rearview mirror. I suddenly realized the lights were for me.

When I pulled the car over, I reached for my license and registration. As I rolled the windows down, tears were still running down my face.

"Do you know why I pulled you over?"

"No, sir," I said between sobs.

"You rolled through the stop sign back there."

"Oh, I'm sorry."

"You don't have to cry about it."

"No, sir, I'm crying because my engagement is off. I had to pick up my dress yesterday. It was the hardest thing I ever did."

As I unloaded my story on the cop, I could see he was feeling uncomfortable.

He patted me on the shoulder and said, "It was his loss. You get yourself together before you get back on the road and try to have a good day."

With that, he left.

Then it dawned on me that crying actually works. I didn't get a ticket. *Note to self, the water works are effective.* Even though that was not my intention, I had to laugh at myself with the outcome.

***

The wedding was supposed to be on the last Saturday in June. My girlfriend Rene, who would have been in the wedding party, invited me out to California so I could get away.

We stayed in a suite at the famed Beverly Wilshire Hotel in Los Angeles. Rene did her best to help keep my mind off the wedding.

When I woke up, I lay on the bed and said, "I knew I was going to be in a hotel room today; I just never expected that it would be with you." We both laughed.

One thing we did not account for is that June 28, 1997, was a popular date for weddings. We ran into wedding parties everywhere we went—in the lobby of the hotel, as we drove down the street, and in a restaurant.

It was becoming a comedy scene. Rene tried to distract me so I wouldn't notice the brides, but to no avail. "Okay, Lord. I'll deal with it," I said aloud.

This was a crazy end to this chapter in my life. I was determined to trust God in the area of relationships. I knew my decision was the right one. I had to believe that I would meet my Mr. Right. I just needed to be patient.

Chapter 24

A Lasting Love

Through my parents' example, I had a front row view of a healthy marriage relationship. They showed me that a healthy relationship does not mean you do not have disagreements, but it does mean you handle those conflicts in a godly manner.

I never heard them call one another out of their names. They did not use derogatory language. Yes, sometimes loud voices, but never disrespectful. They learned the secret to make it last. And now, Mom and Dad were getting ready to celebrate their fortieth wedding anniversary.

Since my parents eloped, they never experienced the celebrations surrounding their nuptials. This was my opportunity to design the wedding I never had.

I loved planning Mom's surprise bridal shower and organizing the ceremony. All my parents had to do was show up. We arranged everything. It was a family affair. All of my siblings, nieces, and nephews were part of the wedding party. My brother Brian officiated the renewal.

As part of the ceremony, I filmed my parents and asked them the secret of their forty years of marriage and almost forty-five years of being together. They both credited their success to their friendship, love, and relationship in Christ. This trifecta was the glue that kept them stuck together.

***

Over the next decade, our nuclear and extended family had numerous weddings and even more babies—not necessarily in that order. Out of wedlock pregnancies were rampant on both sides of my family. Some would say this was a generational curse—the sins of our forefathers and foremothers being passed through the generations.

I understand what people mean when they speak of generational curses. However, the curse implies that individuals do not have a choice in the situation. That is not what I believe.

God, in his infinite wisdom, has given us free will. He does not treat us like puppets, pulling the strings to force us to act in a way he approves. We have every right to live the way we want. However, with that freedom comes responsibility; with this responsibility come consequences. God will never force us to do anything, including choosing him. So I do not believe we have the right to force others to conduct themselves in a way that is suitable to us.

Even though I was sad, sometimes angry, and always disappointed each time I heard about another single member of the family having a baby, I knew I could not force God's standards on them. My assignment was simply to live my life, God's way. However, my family's sexual activity did leave me with questions.

It was fascinating to me that with all of the unexpected pregnancies, none of my family members, to my knowledge, had chosen to abort their babies, even when the pregnancy was a product of rape. *Thank God, because I would not be here today.*

But why didn't they use that same moral compass to keep them from fornicating in the first place? If they insisted on having intercourse before marriage, why didn't they use birth control? Did they ever think about having to raise a child as a single parent? None of it made sense to me.

As news of each pregnancy got out, what I expected happened. Some people talked about the family. A few seemed almost gleeful whenever out of wedlock pregnancies occurred.

I have to admit, I always felt a level of shame and frustration. I had an attitude, of *how dare they put a stain on our reputation by getting her pregnant.* I also believed if I celebrated the pregnancies, in some way, it would indicate that I condoned the sex outside of marriage. However, as I grew and matured in my relationship with Christ, I realized I made the pregnancies all about me.

My emotions stemmed from my pride. I was more concerned about appearances than the well-being of my relatives. I was more concerned about my family's reputation than I was my family. I did not even consider their feelings.

However, once the Lord revealed my true motivation, I had to face the reality that whether it is pride or fornication, it all falls short of God's standard. We are all perfectly imperfect humans. It's just that some of our deeds are done in public while others remain in secret.

As a result of the pregnancies, I learned a lot about grace. John Piper, a theologian stated, "God's grace is both the inclination of the divine heart to treat us better than we deserve and is the extension of that inclination in practical help."[3] God's grace for our family was undeniable. He proved over and over again, his lasting love for us. It was my desire to be better. I needed to become more like Christ.

Naturally, once each child arrived, different ones stepped up to help take care of the babies, including me. I'm so grateful that God gives us a lasting love for these moments.

Chapter 25

I WANT MORE

In 2002, after securing a central office administrative position back in my home school district, I wanted more. I felt the urge to go back to school. In 2004, I was ready and in a position to act on this dream.

I was reminded of a verse in the Bible. "And we know that in all things God works for the good of those who love him, who have been called according to his purpose" (Romans 8:28 NIV). The Lord allowed all my life experiences to align for this moment in time.

My superintendent was in the last year of his doctoral program at Seton Hall. He encouraged me to attend there. He explained that the program was designed for working administrators. I could do the course work and my dissertation within two years. The best part was I could still work my full-time job in the school district. I felt like this was confirmation. It was my green light. I knew I had the Lord's permission to go back to school for my doctorate.

So, with the go-ahead from the Lord and the encouragement of my boss and parents, I applied to the doctoral program and registered to take the standardized test to get into graduate school. Fortunately, they were administering the MAT in two weeks at New Paltz College.

The day of the exam I felt pretty good. I arrived at the State University of New York at New Paltz early so I could get settled into the space. I brought four number 2 pencils with me to the lecture hall. I planned my strategy. There were one hundred questions in fifty minutes. So, I had to answer two questions per minute in order to finish within the allotted time.

After thirty-five minutes, people started leaving. I looked at the clock. I had fifteen minutes left, and I intended to use every minute of it.

On the paperwork, I instructed them to send my test scores directly to Seton Hall.

It took approximately three weeks for me to hear from the college. When the letter arrived, I tore open the envelope.

"We are pleased to inform you that you are conditionally accepted into the Educational Leadership, Management and Policy doctoral program at Seton Hall, conditioned on you earning at least a 50 on your MAT."

Ugghh, I only scored a 48. *Okay, no problem. I'll just retake the test*, I thought.

I took the test again two weeks later. I sat in the same chair. Once again, I used the entire time. *I only need to correctly answer half of the questions. I can do this.*

When the time was up, I submitted my test and prayed that I got at least a 50 on it.

These test scores arrived sooner than the last ones. That had to be a sign. I ran to my room and opened the envelope. I scanned the report. Test 1, score 48. The retake score—wait for it—46.

What? This cannot be right. Lord, I am confident that you said it was time for me to get my doctorate. As I sat there questioning the Lord, I felt a sense of peace, so I devised my plan. Even though I did not have the required score to enter the program, I decided I wasn't going to let that stop me.

Regardless of what my paperwork said, I knew I was supposed to be there, so I went.

I arrived on campus and went to the educational building. I confidently walked in with my certified check in hand. They took my check, so I stayed.

My first semester, I earned a 4.0 grade point average. After successfully completing the first year, I thought I better make sure I was matriculated into the program.

Upon looking into it, the dean learned the story, and saw that I was *not* in the program. He officially accepted me, thus ensuring that there would be no problems when it came to graduation. That following May, after two years, I graduated summa cum laude with my doctorate of education. *Thank you, Lord. You did it again!*

Chapter 26

AM I ENOUGH?

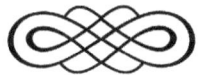

A round 2002, my brother Brian started the concept of HOME groups in our church— Homes Open for Ministry and Encouragement. I became the facilitator for the single women's HOME group. As I led this ministry, I sought God for what to share with them. Many of us were in our early thirties and midforties.

I often relied on book discussions. One book we read was *The Five Love Languages for Singles*. The book, written by Gary Chapman, spoke of how we can have and give love as single people. Chapman has defined the love languages as acts of service, affirmation, gifts, quality time, and physical touch.

For example, I learned that my friend Alaina's love language is quality time. I know, when I plan to visit or call her, I better not have anything pressing that I need to do. One thing she cannot tolerate is when someone rushes their time with her. Alaina loves to spending meaningful time with her friends.

Chapman said we are prone to give love in the way in which we like to receive it. However, if we are speaking a different language than the recipient, they will not be able to identify with our offering as a gift of love.

These differences in our love styles lead to miscommunication and conflict. We feel like we are showing the other person love, but they are feeling nothing. Why? We have not tapped into the person's specific love language.

Because I believe we were designed with community in mind, we have the capacity to have our needs met through meaningful friendships. This group of women, which included my sister, Ann, and friends Alaina, Tawana, Linda, Kathy, and Melissa, became one source of life-giving friendships for me. We celebrated birthdays and even traveled together to retreats, concerts, and other venues.

The Lord used that time to minister to this group of women, but also to me. I felt as if the Lord was asking me, *Am I enough?* I had to accept that this season of singleness may never come to an end. Would I be okay if I never got married? Would I still trust God if my desire to have a mate went unmet? As a person in my midforties, it was a reality I needed to face.

When I finished my doctorate in 2006, I came across a documentary that spoke to my circumstances. It highlighted highly successful, educated, attractive, single, Black Christian women. The question addressed was *Why aren't they married?* I believe most women ask this question at some point in their life.

In the documentary, the producer assembled two different panels consisting of some of her successful, beautiful, Black single friends. They were producers, preachers, actors, models, and other professional women. I could have easily been one of the people sitting there having the discussion with them.

The filmmaker-narrator began the documentary citing a series of statistics. I have to admit, when I saw the data, it was somewhat depressing. They highlighted how Black women are the most uncoupled people in the world. It was as if I were reading the data points from my own life.

That year, I shared the documentary with the singles group at our 2006 retreat. It was a big hit. As a result, the married women asked to view it as well.

That experience was an eye-opener. Many of the married women also related to the documentary. I never considered the number of "married singles" there are, especially in the church. In the vast majority of relationships, the woman was the saved one. Consequently, they often live very separate lives from their spouses. The woman goes to church alone, or with the children, while her man stays home watching the game or fussing over his car. These women deal with a sense of loneliness because, although they are married, their spouse is not doing life *with* them.

The pursuant discussion brought up the topic of masturbation. I had to admit, the thought had never crossed my mind. I attribute this to the fact that I had never awakened my sexual desire. I did not need to masturbate. After all, I could not miss something I had never experienced.

131

I was blessed not to have had any sexual trauma in my life. My parents forbade us from staying over most peoples' houses. This was one way they protected us.

My heart goes out to those who have not been as fortunate. I'm sorry. It was not your fault. However, please know God can heal your broken spaces. Please allow him to touch you in these areas before you embark on a new relationship. You can still enjoy the life you desire. The journey may be delayed, but if you yield your life to Jesus, it doesn't have to be denied.

***

In July 2005, I encountered another "litmus test." My youngest brother, Alan, twelve years my junior, got married. But unlike when my brother Brian married, this time I did not feel jealous.

I drove home from the Seton Hall campus with my camcorder in hand, joyfully ready to support my baby brother on his big day. The wedding, completely planned by Alan, was a wonderful expression of love through word and music.

That day proved to me that I had grown from the twenty-something woman I was at Brian's ceremony. I wasn't perfect, but I was glad I could see progression. The fact that I could show up and engage with others there, confidently moving among the crowd, showed me I was navigating life as a single just fine.

***

After I received my doctorate in 2006, the dynamics at work changed. The superintendent who recommended the program at Seton Hall no longer worked in the school district. Neither did the assistant superintendent who hired me. Now I was the only one in the central office with a doctoral degree.

One of my peers was promoted to the assistant superintendent position. Then my father ran for the school board. He won.

Prior to starting his term on the board, my boss decided to change my job title. This reassignment required me to have to earn tenure all over again. Throughout that month, they made my life at work unbearable. I could no longer deal with the microaggressions and constant scrutiny of my work. I internalized all the stress, and soon my body revealed the score.

Now as I drove up to the building where I worked, my body broke out in hives. I hated going to work. Something had to give. I decided I would quit. Fortunately, I discussed this option with my father before I submitted my letter. He suggested that I request a sabbatical instead.

Because I no longer had tenure, I did not think they would grant the sabbatical, but they did. So, in the summer of 2008, I started a preschool. I called it the King's Kids Early Child Development Center. It was housed at my dad's church.

However, before I left, my boss gave me one last kick out the door. She required me to attend training in Pennsylvania.

The day I rode up to the training site, it was hot. I could see the heat waves as they radiated off the ground. Thankfully, the facility where the training took place had air-conditioning. It was a one-level building with offices, cubicles, a snack area, and two computer rooms. The room where my training took place had eight rectangular tables set up two-by-two, with four chairs at each table facing the front in lecture style. I sat in the front row.

As I scanned the room of about thirty people, it didn't take long for me to count. There were only two of us—two Black people in the class. At least I wasn't the only one this time.

I looked at my watch, 8:35 a.m. I started tapping my pencil, then I checked my email. Whisking into the room, papers in hand, with a computer bag and cup of coffee, the instructor dropped his papers on the table at the front of the room. His face was a hue of red. *Man, this is going to be a week!*

At our first break, I got up to get some tea. The other Black person in the room walked right over to the counter where I was pouring my French vanilla creamer. He was about five foot nine, bald, with deep chocolate skin. He looked around forty years old; but the features that caught my attention were his Taye Diggs smile and eyes!

We exchanged some small talk. He told me his name was Steve. Then it was time to head back to class. Before we went into the room, he asked me if I wanted to eat lunch together. I agreed.

As he walked away, he smiled and spoke with everyone in his path. I took a quick glance at his tight butt, muscular arms. *Hmm!*

Once back in the classroom, I sat back in my seat. I couldn't see his hand. *Was there a ring? Does he have any kids? Where does he live? I wonder if—*

"Paula, do you have anything you want to add?"

"Huh? I'm sorry. No, not at this time." *Girl, focus! I know you don't care about any of this stuff, but don't embarrass yourself!*

When it was time for lunch, we quickly got out of the room. I followed Steve in my car as he pulled into a small local establishment for lunch. We ordered our food, then sat and talked.

"Excuse me, I need to say my grace."

"You can say it out loud," I said. I bowed my head and closed my eyes as Steve prayed over our food. Once he finished, I had to ask. "Are you saved?" After my drama with the guy from IBM, I didn't want to take any chances.

"Yes."

"Me, too. Tell me what led to your decision; how you came into a relationship with Christ." Steve had just started sharing his story when one of the other members from the training class showed up. He ordered his food then came right over to our table.

"May I join you?"

"Sure," Steve said, pushing back a chair next to him before I had a chance to respond.

"Hi," I said. *Where the heck did he come from? Why did he have to sit here? All those other people in the class; he couldn't find anyone else to eat with?*

Steve changed the subject in order to engage the intruder into our conversation. As he reached for the ketchup, I saw his ring finger. *Well, at least one question was answered. No ring!*

Lunch time was over, so we got into our cars and returned to the facility.

The rest of the week, Steve and I ate lunch together every day.

On day three, I introduced him to my family, who had traveled with me. We invited Steve to join us on an outing to Sight and Sound. We saw the production of *David*. The auditorium came alive with the animals, singers, and dancers. It was a powerful witness of God's hand on David's life.

Naturally, I sat next to Steve. Midway through the performance he stretched, then put his arm around me. The palms of my hands got sweaty.

Is he the one, Lord? Is this why I had to come to this training even though I was going on sabbatical for a year in just two weeks? Is this one of those God winks?

Chapter 27

DOUBLE DEATH OF A VISION

Many times, when God gives one a vision, they encounter false starts. It looks like things will work out, but the vision does not materialize. In the case of a double death, it happens *twice*!

Despite my blossoming feelings for Steve, it was a difficult time in my life. It was August 2009, and my sabbatical was coming to an end. The last thing I wanted to do was return to my old job.

The time away from my position in the school district, had reminded me of my "why." I wanted to be around kids. My desire was to become a principal. So, I applied for a principalship in a different district.

I felt really good about my prospects. I had heard that the other candidate did not even have a doctorate. Besides, the superintendent knew my brother Brian. He had worked in the district doing Diversity, Equity, and Inclusion training for years. They required all of their middle school students to go through the training. All faculty were required to attend as well. After all of Brian's training, I thought the district was ready to hire a Black administrator.

The next day, I confidently went into my interview. I had answers for every query. My experience as the director of elementary education in the neighboring district provided me with the curricular background I needed to answer the questions. They told me they would contact me with their response by the end of the next day.

After leaving the interview, I went to the school campus and walked around the building. Like the children of Israel walking around the walls of Jericho, I believed God would knock down the barriers and give me that principal job. *Lord, work it out.*

Once I finished my victory lap around the school, I drove back to the King's Kids Child Development Center to get ready for the afternoon Pre-K class. Right before I got to the door, my phone rang.

"Dr. Palmer, thank you for interviewing with us, but the district has chosen to go with a different candidate."

"May I ask why?"

"Well, they did not think you were a good fit."

"Okay, thank you." In my mind, this was code for *You are too Black.* I hung up the phone, totally dejected. Then I said out loud, "Lord, I know you have a plan for my life, but will you *give me a clue!*"

One week later, I received a call from my superintendent. He told me he wanted me to come back to the district to become the principal at one of the elementary schools. I was so excited. The Lord had answered my prayer.

No, the principalship did not happen the way I thought it would or when I expected. This was another season when I heard *no* twice before hearing yes. But God's timing is always right. Thank you, Jesus!

Part 5

Is He the One?

R esigned to the possibility that I might never marry, I put all my energies into my new principalship. It was energizing. I enjoyed working with the staff and dealing with the children. I had found my sweet spot.

Shortly after my father relinquished the lead pastor position over to my brother Brian, we held a special week of services at our church. The evangelist scheduled to be there had been to our church several times before. I was excited to hear from her and believed she may even have a word of knowledge for me. Every word that she had ever prophesied about my father's ministry had come to pass. I just believed I would receive a blessing from being there.

But God chose to use a different mouthpiece. Evangelist Simmons, a woman that traveled with Mother Graham, uttered the comforting prophecy into my ear. Then she instructed me to write it down.

All I could do was cry with joy. "Lord, I'm amazed how you always send me a word when I need it! I claim this for us," I wrote as I thought about Steve. "I believe the Lord is going to give us a love for one another that will be a witness to the world."

My inclination was to call Steve, but I fought the temptation. There was so much that I wanted to share with him. We had not talked in weeks. He didn't know any of my latest news. *Lord, I know this is our preparation time for marriage, but what is Steve doing?*

I knew one of the major lessons I needed to learn was to allow him to take the lead rather than trying to force a relationship. This is one of the lessons I learned from my several failed attempts at love. It was not easy, especially when I had no idea when, or if, I would hear from him again.

So instead of calling him, I called his mother. She was on my mind anyway—at least, that was the excuse I used to check in on Steve.

"I was thinking of you too," Mama Lou said. "Are you doing okay, honey?" '

Mama Lou was nothing like Mother Jean. Thank God! "Yes I am."

"That's great. I enjoyed your visit last month."

"Thanks again for your hospitality. You made me feel at home." When Steve invited me to his graduation, I stayed at her house. He just earned his master's degree.

Hmm, it just dawned on me the difference in our educational levels. I wondered if Steve was threatened by the number of degrees *I held. Is that why I have not heard from him?*

Regardless, it was good to hear Mama Lou's voice on the other end of the phone. I felt a little closer to Steve.

"Well, Steve is in Chicago."

"That's nice." I tried to sound nonchalant. I wanted to follow up with a million questions, but I stuffed the words.

"Yeah, I think he needed a break. They're giving him a hard time at work. They moved his office closer to his boss's."

God knows I can relate, but I'm also a witness to how quickly God can turn situations around. I knew, from my own experience, that God would create a beautiful tapestry out of all of our life experiences so that he got the credit for what came out of our lives.

Chapter 28

THE CALL THAT
CHANGED IT ALL

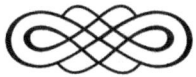

As the year went on, I felt more and more confident that my season was about to change. In September 2009, Prophet Weaver had prophesied that my husband was on his way. I held on to that promise. In fact, I had made a pronouncement at my November 2009 women's retreat. I believed I would be married within the year. I thought Steve might be the person, but time would tell.

Now it was June 26, 2010, the day I went to the Fourth Saturday Conference in Harlem. What I did not realize was that I had caught the attention of someone else.

That Saturday, I wore a black dress with white polka dots. The dress was cinched at my waist, and the bottom of the dress flared out.

"Woah! Is that Paula Palmer?" Elder Juan Perez asked.

"Boy, do you know who you are looking at? Do you know who her father is?" Pastor Ridge asked.

"Yeah, I know."

The next day after his Sunday service, Juan made a call. "Hey, Brian."

"Oh, hey, Juan. What's up, man?"

"I'm interested in asking your sister out. Do you know if she is seeing anyone?"

Brian started laughing. "No. I don't think so."

"Okay. Thank you."

"Juan, a word of advice. Make sure you come correct."

Monday, June 28, marked the start of summer vacation for the teachers but not the administrators. Our summer started with our annual administrative retreat. For many years, that meant getting away for a couple of days at a resort out of the area.

In the past, we had incredible trips to places like Onondaga in Cooperstown; the Sagamore outside of Lake George; and Mohonk Mountain House, right here in the Hudson Valley. Although we still had a retreat, it was scaled down in comparison. We went across the bridge to the waterfront in Rhinecliff, near the Amtrak Train Station.

Alaina and I arrived early Monday morning for the retreat. We planted ourselves in chairs that overlooked the Hudson River. We enjoyed the serenity. The retreat was uneventful but for a phone call.

"Hello?"

"Hello, Dr. Paula. This is Elder Perez."

"Hi."

"I wanted to see if I can take you out on a date."

I nudged Alaina and pointed to my phone. "Sure, when?"

"How about dinner on Saturday?"

"Let's do brunch instead."

"Do you have a place in mind?"

"We can go to Deisings. It's a local restaurant and bakery."

"Sounds good. I'll pick you up around 11 a.m.?"

"I'll meet you at Deisings at 11 a.m."

"Oh, okay. See you Saturday."

"Bye."

I hung up the phone and turned to Alaina. "You are not going to believe this. Juan Perez just asked me out on a date. He wants to go on Saturday."

"What!?"

"Yeah, can you believe it?"

"Oh, wow. How do you feel about it?"

"Numb." I laughed.

Juan Perez and I had known each other for several years. He was an acquaintance from our church circles. He attended a sister church that was in my father's district. All I really knew about him was he was the one assigned to count the money at services. Something about him got under my skin. Shortly after I earned my doctorate, he had referred to me as Paula. I responded, "That's Dr. Palmer to you."

Lord, what is going on? I thought I knew how this story was going to play out. Maybe I was wrong.

Chapter 29

THROW OUT THE LIST

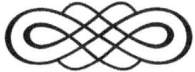

My life turned around after the dream and the prophetic words spoken to my dad. Prophet Weaver told him, "The Lord is preparing your son-in-law, and the spirit of success is upon his life; but his greatest blessing will be in being yoked with your daughter. There is a favor in her life that he needs."

"So, are you ready for your date?" Alaina said. I was glad Alaina was in from the start, so I had someone to talk to.

"As ready as I'm going to be." I tried to act nonchalant, but it felt like a hundred little butterflies were fluttering in my stomach. My emotions rode a roller coaster, waiting for the cart to reach the crest of the rail and then suddenly dropping. Adrenaline surged through my body.

Juan was not what I envisioned. He did not have a lot of the attributes I listed on my "order form" for my future mate. In fact, in many ways he was the exact opposite.

I was always attracted to men that were around my dad's height, but Juan was taller. I always thought I would end up with a man with deep chocolate, or at least brown, skin. He was a light-skinned Puerto Rican man with a mustache, goatee, hair like Jimmy Smits, and a lot of attitudes, mostly negative. Every time I saw him, he was impeccably dressed.

The thing is, we actually knew each other for several years before he asked me out. Despite that, I still knew very little about his personal life. I knew he was a salesman (Perhaps that's what got under my skin). We even worked on some projects together. He hired me to videotape an event that he was in charge of for his mentor and father figure.

Throughout our interactions, I never once considered him a prospect. But in light of the prophecy, my words at the retreat about seven months earlier, and all that transpired since, for the first time the thought entered my mind for consideration.

By Thursday, I started thinking about what to wear. I didn't want to go overboard and wanted to seem calm, cool, and collected. I wanted to look presentable, but not overly prepared for the date.

I settled on white tailored jeans and a lime green shirt. Although the shirt was made of cloth, it reminded me of bubble wrap texture. I didn't want my family to know about the date in case things didn't work out. Considering my track record with relationships, that seemed to be the safest bet. So, I told Juan I would meet him at the restaurant. But that didn't stop my family from finding out.

"So, Paula, we're going to Alan's house for dinner Sunday," Mom said.

"Sounds great. I'll go," I said,

"How are you going to go? Don't you have a date that day?"

"First of all, no. The date is on Saturday. But second, how the heck did you find out?"

"Brian told us," Mom said.

"Brian? How did he find out?"

"Juan called him to ask if you were seeing anyone."

"What? Great, so now everyone knows."

"Where is he taking you?" my mother asked,

"I suggested that we meet at Deisings."

"Oh, that's a good choice.

So, that Saturday, July 3, I met Juan at Deisings. When I arrived, he was at the door waiting for me. He was wearing a salmon-colored shirt and washed-out jeans. When I walked to the door, he opened it and showed me to our seats. He sat across from me, handed me a menu, and asked me to order whatever I liked.

"I know we know each other as Elder Perez and Dr. Palmer, but I'm hoping we can get to know one another on a first name basis."

I looked up at him, still in disbelief that we were on a date.

"I already know a few things about you," he continued.

"Yeah, like what?" I asked.

"I know your favorite book is *The Shack*. You love *West Side Story*. You are a principal, and your doctorate is from Seton Hall University.

"How did you know that?" *How the heck does he know all this stuff? This is kind of creepy. Is he a stalker?*

"Facebook is my friend. You can find out a lot about people online."

"Food's here." I was thankful that the food arrived. As soon as I get home, I'm taking down all that information on my Facebook page!

As I ate my pancakes, eggs, and bacon, Juan continued to sip on his decaf black coffee and talk. "I work for Sprint," he continued. "I'm free the rest of the day. How about seeing a movie?"

"Oh, okay." *Oh, my goodness, what is happening?*

He looked on his phone and discovered that *Knight and Day* with Tom Cruise and Cameron Diaz was playing at the mall, but we still had almost two hours to spare.

"That sounds good," I said.

"Why don't we leave your car here, and I'll drive," he said.

"Okay, but I'll park it over at my job instead. That will be easier."

Since the movie wasn't starting for almost two hours, I decided to take him to the park where I used to work on my dissertation. We parked the car near the water, then got out and began to walk. The last thing I expected was to run into anyone that I knew. The first person we saw was one of my teaching assistants. She was there with her fiancé. I introduced them to Juan. After exchanging some small talk, Juan and I went back to the park bench and talked.

"I know you like pictures. I brought my camera," Juan said.

He took out the camera and snapped a picture.

"So, tell me more about you. Do you have any children?" I asked.

"Yes, I have three—Sara, twenty-two; Mary, seventeen; and Greg, twelve."

Wow, I had seen Juan in church services for over a decade, but I had no idea he had kids or that he was divorced. I chuckled to myself. I never considered marrying a guy with kids until I met Steve. He had two. *Lord, you sure have a sense of humor.*

I looked at my watch. "Oh, we need to go."

We returned to the car and drove to the mall for the movie.

Juan sat on the left of me, probably because he's left-handed. Once the lights went out, and we settled into the movie, he slipped his arm around my shoulder. I did not expect that move.

***

What was it with the day? As much as I wanted to keep it low key, everywhere we went we encountered people I knew.

At the park we saw one of my teaching assistants from my school. Leaving the movie theater, we ran into another one. Then when we went to the restaurant, we saw about eight college students that attended our church. So much for keeping the day inconspicuous.

After dinner he drove me back to the parking lot where I left my car. He parked his car, then got out to open my door, something he had done all day. But this time, he leaned into me as I got out of the car. I don't know if he planned to give me a kiss or not. I didn't wait to find out. I ducked under his arm, ran to my car, rolled down the window, and yelled out, "See you when I see you." Then I drove away.

Chapter 30

WHAT'S GOING ON?

The day after our first date I was scheduled to fly to Charlotte. I had planned to spend the month at Aunt Shelby's house, my mom's youngest sister.

As I rode on the plane, I felt a little giddy, somewhat confused, and perplexed. *Lord, what are you up to? Juan Perez? He never once crossed my mind.*

All this time, I secretly thought that the friendship with Steve would turn into my happily ever after. He was the first man I met who had children that I even considered marriage material. Since I was in my teens, I was holding out for my "A. C. Green" or "Tim Tebow." But after meeting Steve, I scratched that off my list.

Steve had two different baby mommas, but I did not care. He had so many other qualities that I wanted in a mate. He loved the Lord, was family oriented, had deep chocolate skin, and was

153

around my dad's height. Most of all, he was hot! His bulging muscles and rippled abs were evidence of his hours in the gym. His chest was defined, and his behind was just fine. I got along great with his mom and other family members, including the kids. The youngest one was in elementary school, and the other in middle school.

Lord, I need a clear sign. What am I supposed to do? My attraction to Steve was so natural. Juan wasn't my type. *Come on, Lord, you've got to help me out here. If only I could have a clear sign of what to do.*

Aunt Shelby picked me up from the airport. As soon as I got in the car, I began telling her about Juan.

"Yeah, we went out for brunch but ended up spending the whole day together."

"What did you do?"

"We met at Deisings; after lunch we went to the park. Then we saw a movie and ended the day with dinner. He opened the door for me, pulled out my seat, and took the time to find out about what I liked before the date. But when he took me back to my car and opened the door for me, I jumped out, ducked under his arms, ran to my car, started the engine, rolled down the window and said, 'See you when I see you.' Then I burned rubber out of the parking lot."

"Who says that? It was so dumb. He must think I'm an idiot. I was just so flustered I didn't know what to do. I thought he was leaning in to give me a kiss. It was all too much."

As I finished telling Aunt Shelby the story, the telephone rang. The name on my caller ID, Steve! *What is going on, Jesus!?*

I picked up the phone and tried to act like I didn't know who was on the other end, but inside my heart was racing, and the butterflies in my stomach were fluttering.

"Hello."

"Hi, Paula."

"Who is this?"

"It's Steve."

"Oh, hey Steve. How are you? Long time no talk."

He chuckled, and then proceeded to catch me up on what was going on in his life. After exchanging niceties, he said, "Remember when I said when I was ready to marry, I would buy a new house? Well, I just bought a house."

What? I thought, but I didn't say a word. I held my breath and listened intently to the words coming out of his mouth. What was he going to say?

"A couple of months ago, I ran into the mother of one of my son's friends. Her son was on his football team. Well, we started talking and really hit it off. One thing led to another."

"Oh, that's great. What's her name?"

He started laughing. "You're not going to believe this, but her name is Paula."

"No! That's crazy. Tell me more."

"Well, we're engaged. I proposed to her at the Governor's Ball."

"Wow! So, when are you planning on getting married?"

155

"In September. I'd love for you to come," he said.

"This September? Wow. When did you propose?"

"In January," Steve said.

"God, you're amazing!" *Well, Lord, that's my answer. That door is closed. I guess I'm supposed to walk through this one.*

"Why did you say that?" Steve asked.

"I was just asking the Lord to give me a clear sign of what I'm supposed to do. I just went out with this guy named Juan yesterday. I was trying to figure out what to do. Your call has given me clarity."

"You should go for it."

"Yes, I think you're right." When I hung up, I just thought about God's timing. After being on pause for so long, it was like everything accelerated overnight.

Well, Lord, I don't know what you're doing, but if you want me to marry this guy, you have to give me feelings and an attraction for him. Juan was a light-skinned Puerto Rican. He was so light, I know people assumed he was white. He's so outside my picture of a mate. He's nothing like I imagined for myself. Not only that, but he also had three kids! I think it was more about the age of the kids. Juan's kids were older than Steve's.

As I spent the rest of the month in Charlotte, I decided not to call or text him. I just waited for affirmation from the Lord. I needed the time to wrap my head around what was going on. Juan didn't call me either.

The rest of the month, I just began thinking about the possibilities.

Chapter 31

CUPID'S ARROW

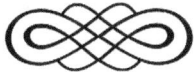

I got back home from Charlotte on Wednesday, August 3, a month after my first date with Juan. Coincidentally, that evening also marked the beginning of our district services. All of the churches that reported to my father convened at Pointe of Praise, our church, for three nights of services.

When I got to the church, I parked in my usual spot by the side door. When I walked in, I could see through the window of the fellowship hall door that Juan was here. He was sitting in the back with Pastor Ridge.

Instead of going straight ahead into the fellowship hall, I turned to my left and entered the sanctuary. I needed to take my position in the choir stand.

That evening, Juan was the speaker. He shared that he was diagnosed with something but was trusting God for his healing.

Honestly, after that, I can't remember much more about what he said.

I just knew that, suddenly, I felt like my hardened heart was pierced by one of Cupid's arrows. My heart turned to mush. The Lord had given me a love for him. The rest of the evening, I just kept watching Juan.

When service was over, I headed directly toward him and gave him a big hug. "Oh, my friend!" I said, hugging him tightly and a bit too long for it to be a casual hug.

Now, what I didn't realize was that my girlfriend Alaina, who is extremely intuitive, observed the whole interaction. When I was alone, she came over to me.

"What was that?"

"What?"

"You know what. I saw that hug!"

A wide grin came across my face. Then, I shrugged my shoulders.

"I see you're still here too?"

I knew full well what Alaina was saying. Normally, I would be halfway to the door before the benediction was over, but noticeably, not tonight.

Instead, I lingered around the crowd, waiting for the opportune moment to speak with Juan.

I knew he had to count money, so I strolled back to the administrative wing (one of the perks of being the preacher's kid and having keys for all the doors).

"Hey, Dr. Paula. How was your trip to Charlotte?" he asked

"It was great. I had a chance to get some rest and hang out with my Aunt Shelby. How was the AIM Conference?" Ironically, Juan's trip to Charlotte overlapped with mine. He went there for the church AIM Conference.

We talked until it was time for him to drive his pastor and wife home.

"I'll call you tonight when I get home," he said.

It took him about an hour to get to his house and call me. That first evening, we talked almost all night.

Thursday evening couldn't come fast enough. I was excited to go to the church service. Juan would be there tonight too.

After the second night of service, Juan asked me to walk with him to his car. He opened the door and let me into the front seat of his red Nissan Altima. Once he sat in the driver's seat, I turned to ask him a question, but Juan leaned over and kissed me on the lips. His lips were soft and moist. Unlike the ten-year-old Paula, I didn't slap him. I didn't run this time either. He kissed me and I liked it! This began our courtship.

Chapter 32

LET'S DO THIS

T he weekend after we officially started dating, my family and I went away for two weeks. I was so grateful to have a cell phone.

"Is she on that phone again?" Dad asked.

"Yeah, I heard it ring at 7:30 this morning."

"I hope she's not driving this relationship. You know how she can be."

"I know."

"Good morning, Mom and Dad," I said.

"Oh, so you're finally off the phone," Mom said. "Were you talking to Juan again?"

"I was." A big grin came across my face. I couldn't conceal it if I wanted to.

"How's he doing?" Mom asked.

"He's great. He's off work for the next month or so."

My parents just looked at each other.

That's how the days went the entire time my family and I were away. The weeks seemed to move slowly, but finally we were heading back home.

My cell phone rang again.

"Hi, Paula."

"Hey, Juan. So, how are you doing?"

"Great. I'm meeting up with the kids a little later. I really miss you though."

"Me too," I said.

"Which way are you guys driving back?"

"Route 84, then we'll pick up the Thruway."

"Why don't you ask your parents to drop you off in Newburgh? I'll bring you home."

"Okay, I will."

As we continued our drive, I waited for the opportune time to ask my father if he would drop me off in Newburgh. At the next lull in the conversation, I jumped in and asked.

"Dad, would you drop me off in Newburgh as we drive through?"

161

"For what?

"I want to see Juan."

"No man wants a woman chasing after him."

"Dad, that's not the case."

"The answer is no."

"Why not? He said he'd drive me home."

"I'm through with this topic," my father said.

I didn't want to overreact, so I said nothing. I wiped away a tear.

In my head I argued, *I'm a grown woman. I didn't even have to ask you.* But, as usual, I pushed the words down. I dared not say them out loud. I had too much respect for him.

When we neared the time we would pass through Newburgh, Juan called again. "Are you coming?"

"No."

"Can you talk?"

"No."

"Call me when you get home."

"Okay, bye." I hung up the phone and rode the rest of the way home in silence.

When I got home, I called Juan, and we planned to meet each other the next day.

"I'll pick you up around nine tomorrow morning. I want to show you something. I also want to introduce you to my kids."

"Okay."

As I lay in the bed, I kept looking at the hands on the clock. I couldn't wait until I saw Juan again. We were in our third week of dating.

***

"Morning, Mom and Dad."

"Morning Paula. Where are you going?"

"Juan is picking me up."

"Wait a minute, we need to talk. Have a seat." Dad had a scowl on his face. Mom sat on the bed and just shook her head. "No man wants a woman chasing after him. Do you know how desperate it makes you look?"

"But Dad, it's not me. Really!"

"Paula, you have been here before. This is nothing new. You are always rushing into things."

"This is different."

"You need to slow this down."

Thank God, the doorbell rang at that moment. I ran to the door to let Juan in.

"Hey," he said.

"Hi, Juan. I'm ready." I pushed him aside and walked toward his car. He shut the front door then followed me out.

"What's wrong?" he asked.

I said nothing. Juan opened the car door, and I got in.

"Where are we going?"

"I want to show you something."

As he drove, my fist and jawline tightened. *I know I acted like a fool before, but why didn't they believe me? They want me to take my foot off the accelerator, but it's not my foot!*

I hated how I felt. The strained relationship with my parents was difficult for me to navigate. I wanted and needed their approval.

"We're here," Juan said.

"Are you picking up the kids? Whose house is this?

"Let's go in."

That's when I noticed the lockbox.

"Juan, what?"

"Well, when we talked the other day, you mentioned that you wanted to buy a house. I found this one."

Oh no! Juan introduced me to the Realtor, who then invited us to walk around the home.

"Is something wrong?" Juan asked.

"I had no idea we were looking at houses."

"What do you think? Can you picture yourself here?" the Realtor asked.

"I guess."

Sally left the house so Juan and I could talk privately.

"Juan! My parents are going to lose it."

"What's wrong?"

I explained to Juan the morning events. After updating him on the state of affairs with my parents, I suggested that we call Brian.

"Hey Brian, I'm in Highland with Juan. It's sort of an emergency. Could you guys meet us at this address? Please don't say anything to Mom and Dad."

"What's wrong?" Brian asked.

"I'll explain when you get here."

About an hour later, Brian and his wife showed up at the house.

"Hey, Brian."

"Hi, Juan. So, what's going on?" Brian asked.

"Well, first let me show you the house," I responded.

Brian and Melody walked around the house. After they looked at the house, we walked back outside. "So, what did Mom and Dad say?" Brian asked.

"Well, that's it. They don't know about the house," I replied.

"What?"

"Yeah, in fact, this morning they told me I needed to stop chasing Juan, and that no man wants a desperate woman."

"So, what you're saying is, they don't know how serious you two have gotten. What's it been, three weeks?" Brian asked.

I nodded my head yes.

"Oh, my goodness, Paula. They're going to have a cow and a couple of calves."

"What should we do?" Juan asked.

"Well, Juan, it sounds like you need to have a conversation with my father."

"I have no problems doing that," Juan responded.

"Without me," I said.

"No problem." Juan looked at me and then put his arms around my shoulders.

"I'll call and make an appointment for next week with him."

It was settled. Juan would take care of it all. His take-charge personality was so refreshing. It made me admire him even more.

"By the way, just in case, my middle name is Cheryi, spelled, C-H-E-R-Y-I."

Chapter 33

MEET MY CHILDREN

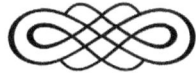

"**C**ome on, Paula. We need to get to Pine Plains to pick up the kids. They know you're coming," Juan said.

As we traveled to get the kids, I thought about Steve. God's plan for my life started to come into focus. Meeting Steve was part of my preparation for now. Prior to meeting Steve and his kids, I never entertained the thought of marrying a divorced father of three. But here we are now. I'm getting ready to meet them.

"How old are the kids again?"

"Sara, my oldest, is twenty-two; Mary is seventeen; and Greg is twelve. We will pick up the younger kids first and then drop by Sara's job to meet her. She works at the mall."

We drove about a half hour to get the kids. When they heard the horn, they ran out to the car. Greg was first. He was wearing jeans, a T-shirt, and glasses. He was almost my height. The middle child brushed her deep brown hair out of her face. She looked more like her father than her brother did. Her skin was beautifully tanned. Her Puerto Rican roots outshined her Polish ones. Juan coined a phrase for his kids. He called them "Poli-Ricans."

As the kids got in the car, their father gave each of them a kiss.

"This is Dr. Paula."

"Hi," Greg said.

"Hello," said Mary.

"She knows Principal Bonnie."

Sara, their older sister, was at work, so we drove to her job at the mall. Juan waved as we entered the store. We were greeted with a halfhearted wave.

"Hey, Sara, this is Dr. Paula"

"Can I talk to her for a minute?" Sara asked.

"Sure, Squirt," her father said.

I turned and looked at Sara. When she faced me, with her brow raised and bulging eyes accentuated by the eyeliner and mascara she was wearing, she stated coldly, "I have a mother, and I don't need no friends."

Okay, wait. Where are the cameras? I must be on Candid Camera. I've never had someone so young speak to me that way. Lord, hold my tongue!

"Sara, I assure you. I'm not trying to replace your mother." *No kid of mine would act so ugly!* I thought.

Juan appeared moments later, I'm sure reading his daughter's body language.

"Okay, Sara, I know you have to get back to work. What time are you off today? Do you want to join us for dinner?"

"No, I have plans."

"Okay, we'll see you some other time." He grabbed my hand, then summoned the other two as we left the store. "I'm sorry," he said. He obviously knew his daughter.

After we ate lunch at Johnny Rockets, we dropped the kids back home. Then Juan drove me back to my house. We took the back way over the mountain.

Lord, I'm so thankful I learned my lesson on dealing with other folks' kids prior to meeting Sara, I thought.

I learned this lesson a couple of years earlier. I had a lunch date with some friends of mine. It was supposed to be a girls' day out, but one of the ladies brought her teenage child. When I was coming up, we were always taught to stay out of grown folks' business. I learned that is not everyone's expectations. The teenager kept interjecting himself into the conversation. The first couple of times, I looked at his mother. She said or did nothing. Finally, I couldn't take it anymore.

"This is an A–B conversation, so see your way out of it," I said. Let's just say, his mother didn't appreciate it. She looked at me with the rage of a mother bear protecting her cub. Our lunch was cut short.

On the ride home, Alaina said, "You can't do that."

"What?"

"Discipline someone else's child."

This concept was so foreign to me. We grew up in a time when neighbors were a part of my parents FBI (Family Bureau of Investigation). They took the African proverb "It takes a village to raise a child" literally. If we were caught doing anything wrong, we would get it by the village member, and again when we got home. Boy, have things changed!

***

"What are you doing on Saturday?"

"Nothing," I said.

"Good, I want you to meet my dad."

"Where does he live?"

"Pennsylvania. I'll pick you up at seven tomorrow morning."

"Seven?"

"Don't worry, you can sleep in the car."

The next morning, shortly before seven, Juan texted to let me know he was at the house. He didn't want to wake the others by ringing the doorbell. My parents knew I was going to Pennsylvania with Juan.

"Good morning."

"Aww . . . These roses are beautiful. Let me put them in the house. I'll be right back." That's how my new love started off the day. It took us almost four hours to drive to his dad's apartment.

After picking up his father, we went to a nearby mall. It was uncanny how much his dad looked like an older version of Uncle Ramon. He had the same jaw line and was balding in the same way. They were also about the same height.

I could see where Juan got his skills. His dad was quite the charmer too. He purchased me a bottle of White Linen perfume. *So sweet.*

As we strolled around the mall, Juan suggested that we look in the jewelry store.

"Let's check in here."

"Okay." *Wow, this guy means business.*

"Let them size your finger, Paula."

After they sized my finger, we left the store. Juan didn't even ask me what I liked.

Talk about déjà vu. Devin brought me to a jewelry store too but with a different outcome. I still can't believe he had the nerve to ask me to purchase my own ring. I'm equally ticked off with myself for doing it!

Chapter 34

IT'S ALMOST TIME

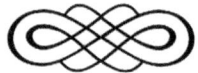

I t was a gorgeous day. The leaves were turning their different hues of red, orange, green, yellow, and brown. I loved the crispness of the air. This was my favorite time of year!

As we drove through the reservoir and back down the mountainous road, Juan spoke to himself but out loud.

"I have almost everything I asked for!"

"Excuse me? What are you talking about?"

"You. I have almost everything I prayed for in a wife."

"Why almost? What didn't you get that you asked for?"

"I wanted a virgin."

I looked at him with a puzzled look, then an annoyed one. "Excuse me, what makes you think I'm not?"

"You are?"

"Yes! Of course."

"Paula, I didn't mean to offend you. I just don't know any girls, inside or outside the church, that waited until they got married."

"Well, I am the answer to your very specific prayer."

Juan pulled the car over to the side of the road. He got out and started walking, waving his hands in adoration and shouting, "Thank you. Jesus! Praise you, Lord!

After a couple of minutes, he returned to the car.

"How did you do it?"

"It wasn't always easy, and I often made mistakes, but the Lord kept me pure through BOUNDARIES." It's an acronym the Lord gave me which stands for:

B	Believe in Jesus,
O	Obey God's Word
U	Understand God's principles
N	No wed, no bed
D	Develop self-control
A	Accountability partners
R	Renew my mind
I	Improve my impact
E	Embrace truth
S	Self love

I believed the guardrails on the side of the road were provided to help protect and guide me through this journey. These boundaries were a demonstration of God's love and care for me.

I love the melody of so many R&B songs. But as I grew in my walk with the Lord, I became more sensitive to what I allowed in through my senses. What always catches my attention first is the melody. However, I realized I needed to also pay attention to the lyrics. Once I tuned into the words, it became apparent that many of the songs I loved were about illicit relationships. A lot of the songs were about adulterous relationships, like in the song by Billy Paul's "Me and Mrs. Jones" and Whitney Houston's "Saving All My Love for You."

It took me a while, but I realized every sin starts with a thought. The more I fed my mind with messages that violate God's principles the more prone I would be to try them. I needed to be mindful of thoughts. My prayer was, "Lord, guard my heart and transform my mind." But that was not enough. I had a role to play in this process. I had to exercise self-control. As Apostle Paul said, I had to "discipline my body and keep it under control" (1 Corinthians 9:27).

I needed to sift what I inputted using my senses through the Philippians 4 filter:

> Finally, brothers and sisters, whatever is true, whatever is noble, whatever is right, whatever is pure, whatever is lovely, whatever is admirable—if anything is excellent or praiseworthy—think about such things. Whatever you have learned or received or heard from me, or seen in me—put it into practice. And the God of peace will be with you. (Philippians 4:8–9 NIV)

I kept myself from getting into all types of sexual sins, including pornography. It is easier to contain the energy than try to bottle it back up after it is unleashed. Once my senses were awakened, it would have been difficult, but not impossible, to contain. The Holy Spirit would have to empower me. I would have to rely on all the "fruit of the spirit," including patience and self-control.

***

Tuesday, August 31, was D-day, the date Juan was scheduled to meet with my dad. Unfortunately, I could not go because it was also the first day the faculty had to return to school.

"I'm meeting your dad in his office at ten this morning. I printed out my presentation and brought three copies."

"Three?"

"Yes, in case your mom decides to sit in."

"Text me when you're finished."

About thirty minutes later, Juan texted me, "DONE!"

I excused myself from the session and went to the hallway so I could call Juan and get the details.

"Hey. How did it go?"

"It went really well. Since you could not be there, your mom decided not to come. When I handed your dad the folder, he laughed. I told him my intention was to marry you.

"What did you have in the folder?" I asked.

"I put in my financials, my resume, and information about the house we saw last week."

"Wow, you weren't playing around."

"Believe me, your dad knows who is accelerating this process."

"Thanks, Babe!"

"Believe me, he knows I'm the one driving this relationship."

"Whew. I'm glad you shared your feelings with my dad. It's important for me to have his approval."

'Well, you definitely have it now."

"Thanks for talking with him. I've got to get back to my training. I'll see you after work."

"Okay, Babe, see you later."

***

"Happy summer."

"Hey, Paula. You look great. Something is different about you," said JC, my head custodian.

"What do you mean?"

"You look at peace, happy. You must have had a great summer."

"I did."

"Oh, I see now. It's a man. Okay, I want to hear about this person that has changed you," JC said.

I took the time to fill my custodian in on my summer romance.

"When do I get to meet him?"

"I'm sure he'll be by the school at some point. You will meet him soon," I said.

"Good for you. It's nice to see this side of you."

"Thanks, JC."

***

That evening Juan and Greg picked me up from my house. We were taking Greg to the indoor skateboard park.

The doorbell rang.

"I got it. Hey, Babe," I said with a kiss.

"You ready?" Juan asked.

"Yes, where's Greg?"

"He's in the car."

"Hmm. Okay. Mom and Dad, I'll be back around 10 p.m."

As we went out to the car, I caught a glimpse of Greg. His head was down, and he sat in a slumped position.

"You don't look very excited about the skateboard park. What's wrong?" I asked.

"Nothing."

Based on his sisters' behaviors and some of the conversations I overheard, I sensed that it had something to do with me.

"Greg, is your family talking about me?" I asked.

Greg nodded. Juan often referred to his ex-father-in-law as Archie Bunker. Juan said he had issues with minorities. Juan thought his ex-wife married him to spite her father.

However, more than loving white people, he loved his money. He did whatever he could to get it and hold on to it. Juan said his ex-father-in-law lost a job because he embezzled money and stole tools from his job. He didn't believe in banks, so he always kept a large stash of cash in the house under lock and key.

Juan said his former in-laws lived in a wacko compound. His ex-father-in-law ruled the roost. Juan often spoke about how his former father-in-law mistreated his wife. He suspected that his daughter, Juan's ex-wife, knew one of his many secrets. Juan's ex-wife had no respect for either one of her parents. With that much hatred and dysfunction within the family, I could only imagine the comments they made about me.

"Are they calling me names?" I asked.

Greg nodded his head up and down again.

"Did they call me a nigger?" I pulled down the rearview mirror so I could see Greg's expressions. He opened his eyes wide, appearing shocked that I figured it out.

"They call you my nigga momma," he whispered.

His pain was obvious. I knew it bothered him. I appreciated that he did not share their sentiments.

"Greg, you know what? They are not talking about me. You know how I know? They do not even know me!" I said it matter-of-factly, without anger or judgment. I knew this was a teachable moment for my future son. I certainly did not want to lash out. First of all, for a Black woman, that was not acceptable. It would fuel even more racist responses from his family. I also knew the importance of Greg seeing the real me and not a stereotype. Black women are often called aggressive, angry B's.

As unfair as I knew it was, I also knew I had to maintain my dignity, self-respect, and more importantly, my Christian witness. I had to show Greg that I was the bigger person. Not only because I did not want him to have experiences with me that confirmed the racist attitudes his family tried to teach him. However, more importantly, I wanted Gregory to understand that, as a Jesus follower, I had to show forth love. That is what would distinguish me from so many others. So, I told Greg, "Remember this day. I promise you, there will be a time when we will be able to eat a meal together."

Juan diverted his eyes from the road to look at me. His eyes showed me that *he* did not even believe that was possible.

"Yes, I meant what I said. I am going to love the hell out of them. They need Jesus. One way they can learn that Jesus is real is by the way we act and, more importantly, the way we react to what they say and do."

We drove the rest of the car ride in silence.

***

The start of my second year as principal was great, but it was hard for me to get back into work mode. Juan volunteered at the school every day. My staff got used to seeing him on the campus helping me with recess or in the lunchroom. I lived in the euphoria of this new relationship. It was hard to break free of the fog of it all.

I sighed and wondered, *Is it me, or are my faculty members feeling the same way about the school year?*

That is why in my weekly email to the staff I ended with, "I don't feel like being here! Is anyone else finding it difficult to get your groove back?"

The staff responded with a flurry of comments.

"You're in love."

"It's Juan."

"If I was you, I'd feel the same way."

"You've got a hot man, no wonder you can't think."

I loved this season of my life.

I was outside waiting for the school dismissal bell to ring when Juan called me. "Don't forget we have to go look at the townhouse after work. I'll be there when you get off."

"Yeah, I'm getting ready to dismiss the kids now. I'll be ready."

I greeted the parents who were outside waiting to pick up their kids, and then the bell rang.

Once all the kids were safely in the hands of their parents, I went back into my office. Almost immediately, two female staff members came in and asked what I was doing for the weekend. I told them we were going to look at a place in Pine Plains. They then said they would let me get ready and reminded me to freshen my makeup.

With a smile on my face I said, "Okay."

Looking in the mirror, I fixed my hair and reapplied some lipstick. As I was getting ready to put on more eyeliner, Lori came running into my office.

"Dr. Palmer, we need you in the gym right away. It's an emergency!"

With those words, I tried to run down the hall, but a couple of staff members were standing in my way.

"Please move. I need to get to the gym!" I started to run. The last time I was summoned like this, I found one of the secretaries at the district office dead on the floor. I remember going to the hospital, seeing her child's grief when the doctors told him the news. *Please, Lord, let this not be a repeat of that. I can't go through that again.*

As I burst through the doors, standing there looking at me appeared to be all of my faculty and staff. It took a moment to comprehend that it was not that type of emergency.

"What's wrong? What's going on?"

"Dr. Palmer. Dr. Palmer. We need you up here. Just take my hand and follow me," my custodian said.

"My heart is in my chest!" I said out loud. The staff laughed.

I took his hand and walked through the crowd up the stairs to the stage where he sat me in a chair front and center.

"Sit right here," he said.

"Surprise!" It was Juan's voice!

"Oh, my God."

It was at that moment that I caught Juan out of the corner of my eye. He was walking toward me from the wings, stage left, wearing a suit jacket and tie and holding a bouquet of roses.

Then he yelled, "Surprise!"

"Oh, my God." I covered my face with my hand. Juan handed me a bouquet of flowers.

"Thank you."

"Now close your eyes. Are they closed?"

"They're closed." The onlookers began to laugh.

"Are you sure?"

"Yes! They are closed," I said.

Digging into his pocket, Juan pulled out a tan ring box and opened it. Then he pulled up his pants leg and knelt beside me. "Now open them."

I gasped, then put my arm around Juan's neck and pulled him into me. The crowd started clapping.

"The one question is, will you marry me?"

"Oh, *yeah!*" I shouted. This was followed with laughter and more applause from the onlookers.

Juan took the ring out of the box and slipped it on the ring finger of my left hand. "Oh, my God! Oh, my God! Oh, my God!" I said with a wide-toothed smile! I looked at the ring on my finger, then hugged Juan again. I kept saying, "Oh, my God!"

Then I turned and pointed to the crowd and yelled, *"You guys are awful!"* The faculty applauded and laughed again.

Juan turned to them and said, "Thank you."

Only then did I realize that Juan had arranged for the proposal to be caught on tape. Sadly, this was another time when a professional videographer should have been secured. The well-meaning camera person was so caught up in the excitement, she missed my entrance into the gym.

"You guys are good. They came in and said, 'Dr. Palmer, we need you in the gym, right now!' So, we're walking, and I say, 'So if we need to be in the gym right now, move, move, move!'" I started laughing again, then I smelled the roses.

"Congratulations! Congratulations," they yelled as they continued to clap.

"How's the ring?"

"He did good," I said as I admired the ring.

"Let's see it, let's see it. Come on," I got out of my chair and walked to the edge of the stage to show off my new prized possession.

"Oh, beautiful! Aww. That's nice"

"I had nothing to do with it," I said. "He picked it out all by himself!"

"I love this man!" I gave Juan another hug.

"Aww."

"I'm trying to get my groove back and this is not helping! You're good!"

"Thank you all," Juan said, extending out his arms. "I appreciate you all helping to make this special."

"Oh, man, you really got me! I thought you were going to propose on my birthday, 10/10/10."

"I know; that's why I changed my plans."

"September 24. I'll remember this date; it's my cousin's birthday."

"We have to get going. The Realtor will be at the house at 5 p.m."

As we drove over the mountains to the place in Pine Plains, I kept looking at my finger. The fairy-tale moment happened. He bought me a beautiful, white gold solitaire ring. The diamond ring, a little over a carat, was clear and sparkling.

"I bought the ring almost a month ago."

"Really?"

"Yes, when I took you to the jewelry store, I had already bought the ring, I just wanted to make sure the size was correct."

"Wait, we were dating less than a month at that point."

"Yup."

"So, what do you think about getting married over spring break? I'll have a week off then."

"I was thinking of December."

"Next December?"

"No, this one."

"Oh, that's too soon. How can I possibly pull together a wedding that quickly? In February, my parents will be celebrating their fiftieth wedding anniversary. I assume we'll be doing something to celebrate their anniversary. Then we have the issue of the time of year," I said.

"Slow down, Paula. Let's just see how it goes," said Juan.

In August, after Juan met with my dad, we decided to rent instead of buy a home. However, I thought it was important that we find a place closer to where his kids lived. Things were happening so quickly, I thought having them adjust to us in a new city would make our initial transition even more difficult. So, Juan asked the Realtor to find a place near the kids in Pine Plains.

The Realtor found the perfect setup. A woman from New York City purchased a townhouse and wanted to rent it. Her asking price fit our budget. The townhouse was a perfect start-up. It was within walking distance of the kids' house and schools. Juan and I signed the lease that evening.

On the way back we stopped by my brother Brian's house.

"Let me see the ring," Melody said.

"May I be in your wedding?"

"You want to be in the wedding party, Di?"

"Yes!"

"Me too!" Brianne said.

"Hmm, okay." The thought of including my nieces and nephews had not crossed my mind, but I liked the idea. Having most of the wedding party be family members would certainly make my life easier. I would not have to explain why I chose some friends over others.

"I wish you guys were there. I was so surprised."

"Yeah, I called her right after the bell rang at the end of the day. She was outside with her parents. I was in the parking lot across the street watching her the entire time."

"I got flowers," Mom said.

"Yes, he gave me roses," I replied.

"No. I said, Juan got me flowers too. He stopped by the church before going to the school to show me the ring he bought and to give me a bouquet of flowers. He wanted us to come, but we were busy working the dinner at the church."

"Oh, that's so sweet. I didn't know."

"Your ring is beautiful!" Ann said.

"Thank you. Yes, he did a great job!"

"So, when are you going to have the wedding?" Dad asked.

"I'm thinking over my Easter break," I said.

"That sounds reasonable," Dad said. I was so happy Dad was fully on board. Since Juan's conversation with him, he had not had a negative thing to say.

After sharing some more about the proposal and the new townhouse we just rented, Juan and I left to see my youngest brother, Alan, and his family. Everyone we saw that night shared in our excitement. By the end of the evening, I knew my color scheme and who would be in the wedding from my side of the family. Now we just needed to decide who was going to be in it from Juan's side.

Juan's relationship with his sisters was interesting to say the least. Navigating these waters proved to be quite the challenge. There were residual negative emotions from when Juan and his siblings were children. His father left his mother for another woman, and then he had another child with her. Additionally, Juan's first wife ostracized him from his family. Juan's mother did not have the luxury of seeing her grandkids whenever she wanted. Naturally, this also put a strain on Juan's relationship with his mother. However, she attended the same church that Juan attended, so there was hope that the Lord would bring some healing to that mother-son relationship.

Mother Perez seemed to like me. However, when she was bothered about something, she showed it all in her face. She would look at you with her side eye. Fortunately, I did not get those looks too frequently.

Juan decided to include his stepbrother, Chris, and his wife, Danielle, in the wedding party. Naturally, he wanted all three of his children to be involved too.

Greg was eager to be his father's sidekick as his junior groomsman. Juan's youngest sister offered to do decorations, but I was reluctant because I had not seen any of her work. However, it all worked out.

Chapter 35

I CAN'T WAIT

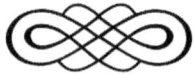

O ur relationship progressed rapidly, but so did my desire to sleep with Juan. I was still committed to remaining a virgin, but I have to admit it was getting to be difficult. The closer we got, the more I was ready to consummate our relationship. I could understand how so many people before me had messed up when they were close to the finish line. However, that was a line I was not willing to cross. Juan knew that and did not want to be responsible for putting a blemish on my record. So, to help us hold out, we moved up the date from April to December. We minimized the amount of time we spent alone. Juan often came to my family's house, rather than me staying at our place in Pine Plains.

Everything fell into place. It was such a blessing. As a principal, I was not allowed to take off days before an extended school vacation. However, after talking to my superintendent, he granted me permission to take off the entire week. I was so excited how the Lord continued to work everything out. We set the date for December 18 at noon.

Even though it was just a couple of months away and in the middle of holiday season, the venue we wanted for the reception was also free. So, we set our plans for December 18 in motion.

Brian designed and printed the wedding invitations. So many people wanted to attend our ceremony that we made it open to any and everyone who wanted to attend. We decided to make the reception by invitation only. Even limiting the numbers, we still had an invite list of close to 250 people.

Juan had three sisters but decided not to ask them to be in the wedding party. He did, however, ask his brother and his wife to come and be a part. Of course, Greg was overjoyed to serve as his father's junior groomsman. Juan knew there was no way his eldest child was going to come. She was loyal to her mother. Mary, however, was the unknown.

Normally, Mary and her dad were very close. He called her his "mini me." But with the announcement of the wedding, their relationship was strained, I'm sure in part because of the pressure she was getting from her mother's side of the family. They had made their feelings about me quite obvious. The fact that Juan chose a Black woman to be his next wife was almost more than they could tolerate. So, the lingering question was, would Mary show up?

***

As Juan and I drove back to Kingston, he asked me if I wanted to have a baby. I didn't even have to think about my response. I was forty-nine years old. The thought of having a geriatric pregnancy was ludicrous. No, I did not want to have a baby. By the time the child would be born, I would be fifty!

Besides, I had watched the impact on my roommate's life all those years ago. Lynn had elderly parents. She lived in constant fear that they would drop dead at any moment. I did not want to put a child through that. Besides, I already had 350 babies. That was enough for me.

That was the population of students at my elementary school. I loved each of these children as if they were my own. I never felt the need to birth a child. It was not a natural craving that I had. With each passing decade, I never thought about my aging womb. I was not the baby-holding type. I had the blessing of helping with my nephew and niece. That was sufficient.

I asked Juan if he wanted to have another child. He told me, not only was he not planning on having more children, but he also wanted to get a vasectomy.

That settled it. Juan scheduled the surgery.

***

It is so interesting to me that, at some point in a parent's life, their child begins acting like the parent. Many seasoned adults experience this reversal of roles. But Juan experienced this from his teenage daughter, who was still in high school.

The weekend I decided to hang out with them, she had a lot of questions for her father. She insisted on speaking to him, alone, in private.

"Paula's not sleeping here, is she?"

"First of all, I'm the parent here, and you are the child. What I do is my business, young lady. But no. She is staying at Lady Ridge's house. Before you ask, we are not having sex either. Paula is a virgin, and she will remain that way until we get married. Which, by the way, will be sooner than later."

"What do you mean?"

"We are getting married on December 18. I would love for you to be a part of the ceremony, May-May. Greg is going to be my junior best man. It would mean a lot to me to have you both there," Juan said.

Mary's look said it all. It was one of anger and loss. She was angry that she was being replaced, while at the same time, Mary mourned the loss of the way things used to be. Even though it was dysfunctional, it was all Mary knew. That was home to her.

The next day, the four of us went to the mall.

"Dad, I'm going to Gala Gowns to look for a dress."

Juan and I looked at each other. Was Mary entertaining the idea of being part of the ceremony?

"Perhaps she's considering your invite to be part of the ceremony," I said

"I hope so."

Mary found a royal blue strapless gown. She looked beautiful in it.

"It looks great, May-May. We can get it now if you'd like."

"Thank you. I'll wear it to my senior formal."

This was a hopeful sign. Juan already knew that his oldest, Sara, would not be there. She barely spent any time with us. Unlike the other children, she aged out of the divorce's visitation agreement and chose to keep her distance. I knew this bothered Juan. He was the happiest he had been, but it saddened him that all his children did not share in his joy.

After shopping, Juan and the kids dropped me home.

***

Now that we had settled on the December wedding date, it was time to get busy on the list of things to do. Fortunately, Juan still had one more week off before he had to go back to work. So he was able to plan everything, except my dress.

"I have my dress already," I said to Aunt Shelby, who was going to be my maid of honor.

"Really? Where did you get it from? What does it look like?"

It's the gown I bought when I was engaged to Devin."

"What? Paula, are you serious? That dress is almost fifteen years old. You'll look ridiculous wearing it. I'm sure it's out of style," she said.

The style of the dress had never crossed my mind. I had not looked at it since I brought it home. It was still tucked in the back of my closet.

After we hung up, I pulled out the dress. Aunt Shelby was right. It had puffy shoulders, a lot of sequins, and lace. There was no way to make it work. Since my old gown was not a viable option, I started searching for a new dress.

It took a couple of days, and several bridal magazines, but I finally found a beautiful ivory strapless, lace trumpet wedding dress designed by Oleg Cassini. However, before settling on this dress, I wanted to try it on.

That weekend, when I was with Juan, Greg, and Mary, we shopped for the wedding. "Mary, would you come with me to David's Bridal?" I was hopeful that if she was involved with the plans, she would decide to be a part of the ceremony. Mary agreed to come.

Juan dropped us off at the bridal shop. Then he and Greg went to the tuxedo shop to figure out what the guys would wear.

"Do you think your dad will like it?"

"Yeah, it's beautiful."

"Great. I think this is the one." I was hopeful that I had found my dress, but I wanted my parents' stamp of approval before purchasing it.

By the time we finished, Juan and Greg were back. I was so thankful things were coming together. Now to figure out what the bridesmaids were going to wear.

Later that week Juan, my parents, sister, nieces, and I traveled to David's Bridal in Albany to pick out the bridesmaid dresses. That was the day I learned about Juan's shopping skills. Would you believe, he was the one who selected the girls' dresses! They were a beautiful red, my favorite color. What Juan did not know was how much the dresses complimented the gown I had chosen.

For the third time that week, I traveled back to David's Bridal. This time I was with my sister, mom, and dad. Today was the day I was scheduled to order my dress.

When I walked out of the room with my ivory gown, I turned and looked at the mirror and said, "Yes, this is it." I had a broad smile on my face.

"That's beautiful, Paula," Dad said.

Mom shook her head and then asked, "Why aren't you wearing white?"

"Well, when I saw the dress in the magazine, it was ivory. I can't even imagine the dress in white."

"Yeah Paula, but you should be in white."

"Why? The purity thing? Everyone that knows me knows that I'm still a virgin."

My father could see that we were each getting a little emotional. "Paula, why don't you just try on the same dress in white. It will be easier for you to make up your mind."

The attendant found the dress and brought it for me to try on. I have to admit, my mom was right. The white dress was equally as beautiful. So while we were there, I selected my shoes, a tiara, a lace jacket, and a cathedral length veil to go with the gown. It was perfection.

***

Juan moved into our apartment in Pine Plains at the beginning of November. He got his best man, James; his sister, and her boyfriend; one of my cousins; and a few of the guys from the church to help him move. Even though I wasn't moving in until after the honeymoon, I also began bringing things to our new home.

The time was moving fast. The weekend our furniture was being delivered was the same weekend as our annual women's retreat. That Friday, Juan drove me to the very same hotel where a year earlier, I had declared that I would be married.

He drove me to Amtrak so we could pick up our speaker who traveled in by train. As she got in the car, we could not wait to share with her our love story. She was so excited to hear how God brought the two of us together. By the time we reached the venue, she had a verbal invite to the wedding!

After dropping the speaker and me off at the hotel, Juan went back home. This weekend was the last time I hosted the retreat as a single woman. Our first night, after our session, we all crammed into our hospitality suite. That's when the women grilled me about the upcoming nuptials and honeymoon. They knew what a big deal this was going to be for me.

"So, what are you nervous about?"

"Making the transition with the kids. I know it has been difficult for them," I said.

"No, about the honeymoon?"

"Oh. Well, if it will hurt. Would you believe, I actually met with Dr. Barnes, my gynecologist. Whenever I went for my Pap smears, he had to use the smallest instruments on me. I met with him to find out if we would be okay. He assured me that the body will do, what the body does." The rest of the women laughed.

"You may need to use some lubrication, Paula, but you'll be all right," Mom said.

I knew I would be, but it was definitely a thought.

Chapter 36

NEW START, NEW SEASON

I could hardly sleep. The day I longed for, for over three decades, was finally here. I was getting married. Although it was December 18, it was uncharacteristically warm outside. The sun was shining, the ground was absent of snow and ice. My white gown hung on the hanger, ready to transform me into a bride.

Juan and all the groomsmen met at my brother Brian's house. They looked sharp in their black tuxedos. The red ties added a splash of color, reminding us that we were in the Christmas season.

Greg was there too. He was so excited about his tux that he asked his dad if he could wear it to his winter formal the following week. Not even his sisters' absence could take the smile off his face.

My mom, my sister Ann, Aunt Shelby, my nieces, and I arrived at the church a few hours earlier to get dressed. I felt like a princess with her attendants. The professional videographer and her team captured it all.

The photographer was freezing moments in time as my mother and Aunt Shelby pulled up my gown over my curves. Tissue paper, empty boxes, and hair pins were strewn on the women's lounge floor as the makeup artist and hairstylist transformed me into Cinderella for the day.

Once my mother and Mother Perez lit their candles and were seated, the ceremony commenced with a slideshow to "I Found Love," performed by BeBe and CeCe Winans. The applause signaled the end of the presentation.

Juan, my groom, was announced by a dramatic liturgical dance. The college girls, some of whom were at the restaurant when Juan and I had our first date, twirled and spun their flags to declare that the groom was coming. It was a dramatic entrance fitting of my king.

The audience turned around to look at the back doors to see the rest of the wedding party, but to their surprise, the doors remained closed. Instead, led off by Juan's son Greg, our junior best man, and my sister Ann's daughter, the party entered from the front stage doors. My nieces and nephews took their job seriously. Alan's daughter, my flower girl, refused to walk down the aisle when she saw the approximately five hundred well-wishers. So Alan went to the back of the church and carried her down the runner.

As the organist played "Here Comes the Bride," the doors slowly opened, revealing me in my white gown and cathedral train. This was a sign of my purity and the thirty-three-year vow I had made to my father and my Lord.

Now linked to my father's arm, I was prepared to step into my new season as Juan's wife. I was ready. It was God's perfect timing.

I felt like I floated down the carpeted aisle. The open door revealed a winter wonderland. Snowflakes danced on the walls. The poinsettias lent to the feeling of Christmas. The lights twinkled in the tulle-wrapped railings. As my dad and I processed down the aisle, I took it all in.

Dad chose not to perform the ceremony. He left that honor to my brother Brian and Juan's spiritual father, Pastor Ridge.

As my brother asked, "Who gives this bride?" my father answered, "Her mother and I do." Immediately, several of my girlfriends, led by Alaina, stood, and shouted, "*We do!*"

In a way, they were correct. My journey was aided by family and good friends like Alaina. The path was filled with sorrow, joy, and pain.

Although it took a long time for me to get here, I would not change a thing. I'm thankful for the gift of my single years. I learned and grew a lot in my singlehood. I discovered God's purpose for my life. I impacted a lot of people. But only God knew when I would be ready to receive, and enjoy this new season, of being a wife, lover, mother, and purpose partner. Now was my time.

That evening, as I lay next to my husband in our honeymoon suite, I reflected on God's timetable. I smiled as I thought about how God's timing was, and always will be, better than mine. I was finally in the arms of my forever love.

Now, as my husband and lover gently caressed my body, arousing feelings and emotions that I had never experienced, I leaned into them without fear, shame, or regret. I allowed myself to totally surrender to Juan, knowing he was completely mine and I was completely his.

As he loved on me, an overwhelming joy bubbled up within both of us. The explosive bursts caused me to scream with ecstasy. The realization that this was going to happen again, and again, and again that night, and for the rest of our lives, made me grin! Yes, my journey to this point was delayed, but it was *not* denied. And oh, was it worth the wait!

Final Thoughts

Thank you for joining me on this journey. Before we leave, just a few more thoughts.

RECAP: LETTER TO
MY SIXTEEN-YEAR-OLD SELF

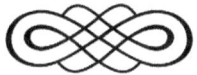

Y ou will spend thirty-three more years waiting for your soulmate to arrive, but take heart. It will be worth the wait. Through your season of waiting, you will question your beliefs, but God's love will surround you, and because of your own experience with him, you will reconfirm that you will follow Jesus all the days of your life. You will realize that you are serving God, not to please your parents but to please your heavenly Father.

You will live through all those years when your partner will be a camera lens rather than a man. Your love of videography will allow you to be in those family moments, yet not be in those moments. You will have times when you feel lonely but not alone.

Your faith will carry you through the years. When the teacher questions your intelligence, you will work hard to prove her wrong. When they don't call you for your first job, your faith will have you pick up the phone and ask the manager when you should start. Dumbfounded, they will tell you to come in on Saturday. That faith lesson will follow you through all your years. You will not settle for no. This faith walk will encourage you to step out and trust God when others give up.

Your first love will not be your last. When he leaves you, the pain will stay for a while, but you will overcome and remain friends. It will hurt when others marry long before you. But you will throw yourself into your work with kids and other single women.

You will teach, start the King's Kids community program, and become a school administrator. Your journey will bring you full circle to where your kindergarten teacher belittled you. You will return twice: first as a teacher and then as principal.

Along the way you will do a *lot* of stupid stuff, like "loan" $5000 to a male friend and buy your own engagement ring (Girl, should have had a clue right there!).

The testimony of the Lord keeping you will cause you to be prideful. When you realize it, you will correct your attitude. It was only God's grace that kept you from being taken advantage of or molested. It was the Lord that kept you until you were forty-nine years old.

As you traverse through life's many doors, you will remember the hurts and embarrassments, but you will use them to fuel you to never give up.

A MESSAGE TO PARENTS

We have such an awesome responsibility as parents. Be strong. You and your kids will mess up. But always remember, God's grace and mercy is new every morning. Ask God to forgive you, and most importantly, forgive yourself!

I encourage you to talk openly about sex in your home. If you choose not to, your children will be prone to learn about sex from unreliable sources like their peers. As you discuss the joys of sex, be sure to include God's perspective. Too many times in the church, sex has been taboo. Remind your children that it is wonderful, but meant for the confines of a loving marriage relationship.

As you train your children, support each one's talents and interests. Naturally your training will include godly principles, but it is important to nurture the gifts and special skills that your child was born with. Teach them to love Jesus. This is what it means to train a child in the way they should go. Help them to discover their purpose, their "why."

Your FBI (Family Bureau of Investigation) must remain active. Monitor the type of media that your children intake. Remember to teach them to run everything they watch and listen to through the filter of Philippians 4:8–10. Learn how to check their devices. Remember a lot of content, including pornographic material, comes through their electronic devices.

I suggest that you not be so quick to kick out your eighteen-year-old. I'm not saying allow them to live with you indefinitely rent-free. Require that they pay their weight as part of the family unit.

If you are creating a blended family, remember your mate's kids are not your children. As much as they say they are, there is something about the parental bond that causes them to run to their children's defense. Follow your mate's lead. When you disagree about their handling of the children, discuss it in private.

Most importantly, remember to love your children. They will mess up. We all do. However, that's why we have erasers. Remember mistakes are attempts at learning. It is important that they learn from their missteps and do better. They should know that God forgives and forgets, and they should forgive themselves as well. That's what grace is all about. Even though we may screw up, God still loves us.

MESSAGE TO SINGLES

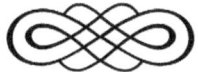

I know there are many times when you feel all by yourself. Please know, there are a number of people that are also living in a God-honoring way. Remember his grace and mercy are new every day. If you struggle in this area, remember, there's always tomorrow. If you fall, get up and try again.

For those of you who are on the path of celibacy, keep going. The Holy Spirit wants to lead you and guide you into all truth. He will give you the power to resist the devil. Don't compromise your convictions.

When you find "the one," get married as soon as you can. Long engagements will increase the likelihood that you will fail in the area of sex. The devil doesn't take a day off. If you are not careful you, will fall.

Please, reach out to me if you are on this celibacy road. I want to support you. Join the "You Are Not Alone" group. Together, in community, we can encourage and support one another.

Acknowledgments

In the cemetery there is buried the greatest treasure of untapped potential. There is a treasure within you that must come out. Don't go to the grave with your treasure still within YOU.

During the COVID lockdown, I heard that quote by Dr. Myles Munroe. It made me stop and ponder; with no birth children of my own, who would share my story? After years of procrastinating, on my sixtieth birthday, I made a commitment to write this memoir before turning sixty-one. This is proof, with the Lord's help, that I did it.

Penning this book has been an amazing experience. From the very start, God supplied my needs from places I never expected, through people I didn't even know, in ways I never even thought possible. With each divine appointment, God whispered to me, I've got you. I am walking with you through this process.

I came across Anna David's podcast about writing memoirs. That led me to join her writing group, the Launchpad Inner Circle. That very first day, when I logged into the group, in October 2021, Lord, you had a "sister" there to welcome me, host Heidi Le. It was her last week facilitating the group, but her job was complete. She was the green light I needed to stay in the group.

Jill Carlyle, then Tim Gager, and on occasion, Barbara Legere became the next leads of this amazing group. Each of you contributed to my growth as a writer. Thank you.

To each of the members of the Launchpad Inner Circle—and in particular: Kimberly, Mike, Amanda, Shuna, Chris, Margie, Sara, Joanna, Heather, Dar, LaTonya, and Jenna—thank you for taking the time to critique my work. You always shared your feedback with a spoonful of sugar, which made it easy to swallow. Ultimately, your words of wisdom improved my work. Your input was invaluable.

Listening to Chrystal Evans Hurst introduced me to Kia Stephens, founder of the Entrusted Women's Facebook Group. In this group, the Lord led me to Luverta Reams, Alexis Goring, Libby Gontarz, Lovelina Atenaga, Janice Johnson Burton, and Pat Weatherspoon Hall. Thank you, women of God, for everything!

Rob Fitzpatrick and the Help My Book communities, thank you for the beta reader tool and the weekly writing accountability groups. Marjorie Turman Holman, thank you for your thorough insights.

To my FT church family and "the well" morning group, thank you. Each day for over a year, you circled this project in prayer. Your prayers propelled me to finish my assignment. I'm eternally grateful for your love and encouragement.

To my aunt, thank you for the hours that you spent reviewing the pages for me. Thank you to each of you who read early drafts of this memoir and then challenged me to be more transparent. I know this book is better because of you. On the other hand, now a whole lot more folks know my business! Hmm, should I thank you for that?

To my close friends, you know who you are. Over the years, we've laughed, cried, and supported one another through various times in our lives: deaths, births, graduations, and weddings. I love you to life! Thank you for being a friend. May God continue to bless you and give you the desires of your heart.

Finally, to my family. I am here because of you. You birthed me. You loved me. You molded me to become the person I am today. Thank you for allowing me to share your stories too. I love each of you. You added the juicy tidbits to my story.

To each of my siblings, nieces, nephews, and extended family members, let's always remember we are here because of God. We have a purpose to fulfill. May everything that we do bring glory and honor to Him.

To my husband, my lover, my friend, my pastor, and my purpose partner, God brought me to you on Saturday, June 26, 2010. I am so grateful that I did not miss that appointment. As the prophet said, the spirit of success is on your life. I'm forever grateful for your impact on mine.

Thank you for putting up with me over this writing year. Your belief in me reassured me that I could do this. I believe all the prophetic words you have spoken about this book. Babe, I love you. You have taught me what love really means. Now, let's do this!

Resources for Your Journey

I want you to be successful in your relationship journey. Whether you are married or a wife in waiting, I want to walk alongside as you as you honor God in your relationship choices. Scan the QR code or visit my website to learn about new products and additional ways we can connect:

<u>https://drpaulacperez.com/resources-for-you</u>

Bonus Content

Scan the QR code to view pictures and
video from some of the events in my life.

ENDNOTES

[1] Harris, Kat. *Sexless in the City: A Sometimes Sassy, Sometimes Painful, Always Honest Look at Dating, Desire, and Sex* (Zondervan, 2021) 140.

[2] McDowell, Josh. *Why Wait? What You Need to Know about the Teen Sexuality Crisis.* (Thomas Nelson, April 30, 1994).

[3] https://www.desiringgod.org/interviews/what-is-grace accessed September 9. *"What is Grace?" An interview with John Piper*

About the Author

Dr. Paula is an educator, leader, speaker, writer, youth pastor, and pastor's wife committed to teaching, equipping, and challenging people to live life triumphantly.

She earned her doctorate in Educational Leadership, Management, and Policy from Seton Hall University. Currently she is an adjunct lecturer for the State University of New York at New Paltz.

In December 2010, Dr. Paula married her husband, instantly becoming stepmother to three young adults. Since 2015, she has served alongside her husband, Pastor J. Perez, at Faith Temple, a church in upstate New York. Dr. Paula took early retirement from her principalship to enter full-time ministry in 2018.

Dr. Paula and her husband are certified *Saving Your Marriage Before It Starts* coaches. Together they provide training for singles, as well as relationship support and coaching to couples.

To book Dr. Perez for an event, email info@drpaulacperez.com. Check out her website and social media links listed on her digital card: http://meetdrpaula.com.

Delayed Not Denied

A Christian Relationship Guide

Based on the memoir,
49-Year-Old Virgin: Delayed Not Denied

Dr. Paula C. Perez

Using her life and her family's experience, Dr. Paula reminds you that you are not alone, regardless of your experience. Whether you are still a virgin, waiting on God to send you your mate, or you've been molested or raped, God can restore you and bring you to the other side.

This interactive workbook guides you through a scripturally based, reflective process that will help you examine your own relationships. In it you will find helpful tips that will help you remain celibate until marriage. Even though you may be delayed, you will not be denied. Like Dr. Paula, you will see that God's timing is always better than yours.

Get your copy of *Delayed Not Denied:*
A Christian Relationship Guide.